Introduction

This book is a compilation of all the 'Word of the day', 'Verb of the day', and 'Vocabulary of the day' posts on the Facebook page Learn Urdu. I have arranged all the posts in this book in chronological order from the past 8 years. They are not all just plain and simple word-with-sentence posts. Many of them have insightful notes on Urdu grammar and structure. They are an interesting read for language enthusiasts in general. Hope you enjoy!

Learn Urdu
7 March 2012 ·

Word of the day: ziddi - stubborn.
Usage: tum say baRa ziddi insaan meñ nay aj tak nahi dekha.
Translation: I have never seen such a hugely stubborn person like you until today.
Literally: you from bigger stubborn human I (nay) today till not seen.

Grammar:

'tum say baRa' means 'bigger/older than you'. Some similar examples are 'mujh say chhoTa' (smaller/younger than me). The meaning is ambiguous until you add 'in height' (kadd mayñ) or 'in age' (umar mayñ). 'vo mujh say umar mayñ baRa he' means 'he me-from age-in big is' (he's older than me).

Vocabulary:
aj tak _____ until today
kal tak _____ until tomorrow
shaam tak __ until evening
subah tak ___ until morning
dopeher tak _ until afternoon
diigar tak ___ until late-afternoon. (this is the time roughly from 3 PM to 6 PM)

Learn Urdu
9 March 2012 ·

Word of the day: ijaazat - permission.
Usage: mujhay aap ki ijaazat chahiay.
Translation: I need your permission.
Literally: to-me you of permission wanted.

Boost Unavailable

3

4 comments

Learn Urdu
10 March 2012 ·

Word of the day: izzat - respect.
Usage: vo baRoñ ki izzat karta he.
Trans: He respects his elders.
Literal: He elders (gen.) of respect does is.... See more

Boost Unavailable

4

Learn Urdu
11 March 2012 ·

Word of the day: chup rehna - to stay quiet. (compound verb).
Usage: Hamza aksar chup rehta he.
Trans: Hamza often stays quiet.
Literal: Hamza often quiet stays is.

In comparison, we can take a look at 'chup hona' which means 'to be quiet'. hamza aksar chup hota he - hamza is often quiet.

Boost Unavailable

2 1 share

Learn Urdu
12 March 2012 ·

Verb of the day: naachna - to dance.
Usage: bachchay baarish mayй naach rahay thay.
Trans: Children were dancing in the rain.
Literal: Children rain in dance ing were.

Grammar:
To be able to dance - naach sakna
To have danced - naach chukna
To return from somewhere after dancing - naach aana
To leave after dancing - naach jaana
To suddenly start dancing - naach paRhna
To dance for oneself - naach layna
To dance for someone else - naach dayna

Note that all these compounds can be added to the root of any verb as far as logic dictates.

For example 'so lo' (sleep for yourself) is logical, but 'so do' (sleep for my benefit) doesn't and isn't even used.

Let's discuss these compounds in the comments below. Try to make sentences involving them.

Learn Urdu
12 March 2012 ·

Word of the day: kabhi nahi - never (lit. anytime not)
Usage: meñ kabhi nahi rouñ ga.
Trans: I will never cry.
Literally: I anytime not cry (future tense) will.

Grammar:

______ rona - rouñ ga ______

The future tense is made by taking the stem of the verb, that is the part without the 'na' ending, and adding 'uñ', 'o', 'ay' or 'ayñ' to it. 'ga', 'gi' and 'gay' (masculine/feminine/plural) are the future tense of 'huun' (am), 'ho' (are), 'he' (is) and 'heñ' (are).

Examples:
meñ khaauñ ga - I will eat.
tum so'o gi - You will sleep. (speaking to a female)
tum ro'o gay - You will sleep. (speaking to a male)
ap jaa'ayñ gay - You will go. (speaking to a male formally or to a crowd)
ap aa'ayñ gi - You will come. (speaking to a female formally or to a crowd of women)
ham dekhayñ gay - we will look.
vo bhaagayñ gay - they will run.

Learn Urdu
12 March 2012 ·

Adjective of the day: bura - bad (buri feminine, buray plural)
Usage: jhooT bolna buri baat he.
Translation: Lying is bad.
Literally: lie to-tell bad talk is.

Note: 'baat karna' means to talk and 'baat' is also the noun 'talk'. However, here 'baat' is being used to mean 'thing', "lying is a bad thing." This feature of using 'talk' to mean 'thing' is found in most South Asian and Iranian languages of Indo-European origin. It is, surprisingly, also found in Japanese, far from this region. 'sonna koto wa arimasen' in Japanese translates directly to the Urdu 'esi baat nahi he' (It's not like that. lit - like-this talk not is).

Learn Urdu
13 March 2012 ·

Verb of the day: sikhaana - to teach (synonym paRhaana)

Usage: vo ustaad ek gornamant kaalij mayñ paRhaata he.
Translation: That teacher teaches in a government college.
Literally: That teacher one government college in teaches is.

Usage: mayñ ap logoñ ko urdu paRhaa raha huuñ
Translation: I'm teaching you people Urdu.
Literally: I you people (gen. pl.) to Urdu teach ing am.

Boost Unavailable

2

1 share

Learn Urdu
14 March 2012 ·

Word of the day: rang - colour

Usage: dhanak mayй saat rang hotay heй.
Trans: There are seven colours in a rainbow.
Literally: rainbow in seven colours exist are.

Note: A synonym for dhanak is 'kos e kaza'.

Boost Unavailable

1

Learn Urdu
15 March 2012 ·

Word of the day: tayzi say - quickly
Usage: yay kaam tayzi say karna he.
Translation: This work has to be done quickly.
Literally: this work quickness with to-do is.

Grammar:

In Urdu, the effect that English gets with the 'ness' suffix, is created by mostly the 'i' suffix added to the end of an adjective.

lambaa (long) ______ lambaai ("longness" - length),
uunchaa (high) _____ uunchaai ("highness" - height),
chawRaa (wide) ____ choRaai ("wideness" - width),
achhaa (good) ______ achhaai (goodness)
buraa (bad) ________ buraai (badness)
tanhaa (lonely) ______ tanhaai (loneliness)
khaamosh (silent) ____ khaamoshi ("silentness" - silence)
rangeen (colourful) ___ rangeeni (colourfulness)
buzdil (coward) ______ buzdili ("cowardness" - cowardice)

Learn Urdu
16 March 2012 ·

Word of the day: dard - pain
Usage: mayray payt mayй dard he.
Translation: I have a stomach ache.
Literally: My belly in pain is.

Vocabulary - Parts of the face.

Face - chehra
Head - sar (sar dard - headache)
Forehead - maatha
Eyebrows - bhawayй
Eyelashes - palkhayй
Eyes - aankhayй
Nose - naak
Mouth - muuй
Lips - hont
Teeth - daant
Cheeks - gaal
Ears - kaan (both singular and plural)

Learn Urdu
17 March 2012 ·

Word of the day: sach - truth

Usage: sach bolo, kya kar rahay ho vahaaй?
Translation: Tell me the truth, what are you doing there?
Literally: truth talk, what do ing are there?

Note: this is talking to a man. For a woman, use 'rahi' instead of 'rahay'.

Learn Urdu
17 March 2012 ·

Vocabulary of the day: Parts of the body.

Body ______ badan/jism
Neck ______ gardan
Shoulder ___ shaana
Chest _____ seena
Back ______ kamar/peeTh
Belly ______ payT
Navel _____ naaf
Thigh _____ raan
Leg _______ Taang
Knee ______ ghuTna
Ankle ______ ayRhi
Foot _______ pauй
Finger _____ ungli
Thumb _____ anguuTha
Arm _______ baazu
Hand ______ haath

Learn Urdu
18 March 2012 ·

Word of the day: kiuйkay - because

Usage: meй aaraam karna chahta huuй kiuйkay mujhay bukhaar he.
Trans: I want to take some rest, because I have a fever.
Lieral: I rest to-do want am because to-me fever is.

Learn Urdu
17 March 2012 ·

Verb of the day: sharmaana - to be shy

Usage: dulhan dulhay kay saamnay sharmaa rahi thi.
Trans: The bride felt shy in front of the groom.
Literal: bride groom of front shy ing was.

Another form that is used is 'sharam aana' (shyness to-come)
mujhay sharam aati he - I feel shy.
tumhay sharam aati he? - Do you feel shy?

When you use this as a question about someone else in the negative, it's meaning turns towards shame rather than shyness.
tumhay sharam nahi aati? - Aren't you ashamed?

Grammar: Note that dulha means 'groom' and 'dulhan' means 'bride'. 'dulhay' is in the 'post-positional case'. This means that it is being followed by a post-position such as kay, mayñ, par, ko, ki, ka etc. I have been calling this the genitive case, but I would be calling it the post-positional case from now on.

Learn Urdu
19 March 2012 ·

Word of the day: ganda - dirty/bad (ganday, gandi)

Usage: mayray kapRay kiichaR ki vajah say ganday ho ga'ay heñ.
Lit. my clothes mud of reason from dirty become went have.
Trans: My clothes have become dirty because of the mud.

Usage: gandi bachchi!
Lit. Bad girl!

Usage: ganday bachchay!
Lit. Bad boy!

Learn Urdu
18 March 2012 ·

Verb of the day: rakhna - to put/to place

Usage: chae mayz par rakh do, kiuñkay abhi garam he.
Trans: Put the tea on the table for me, because it is hot right now.
Literal: tea table on put give, because now hot is.

Note that Urdu makes a distinction between an object being hot and the weather being hot in general. 'ye cheez garam he' (this thing is hot), but 'aj garmi he' (it is hot today).

Grammar: rakhna declension

rakho! Put!
meñ rakhta/i huuñ. I put.
tum takhtay/i ho. You put.
vo rakhta/i he. He puts.
ham rakhtay/iiñ heñ. We put.
vo rakhtay heñ. They put.
ap rakhtay/iiñ heñ. You (pl./for.) put.

meñ rakh raha/i huuñ. I am putting.

meñ rakhta/i tha/i. I used to put.

menay rakha tha. I put. (simple past)

Learn Urdu
19 March 2012 ·

Verb of the day: jaagna - to be awake

Usage:

Ali: (Mike kay saath phone par) Mike, tum jaag rahay ho? so rahay to nahi thay?
Mike: nahi Ali, mayñ jaag raha huuñ. sunao!
Ali: kahiiñ baahir chaltay ho mayray saath? kuch khaatay heñ.
Mike: Theek he. mujhay das minaT do. tayaar hota huuñ.

Translation:

Ali: (On the phone with Mike) Mike, are you awake? You weren't sleeping, were you?
Mike: No Ali, I was awake. Tell me!
Ali: Do you want to go somewhere outside with me? Let's eat something.
Mike: Okay. Give me ten minutes. I'll get ready.

Literally:

Ali: (Mike of next-to phone on) Mike, you awake ing are? sleep ing (to) not were?
Mike: no Ali, I awake ing am. tell!
Ali: somewhere outside walk are me next-to? something eat (we) are.
Mike: Fine is. to-me ten minutes give. ready be am.

Language:
Note the 'to' in the first sentence, "so rahay to nahi thay?" This 'to', when used in a negative sentence, gives the impression of hope. Observe the contract:
tum so rahay to nahi thay? (i hope you weren't asleep?)
tum so rahay nahi thay? (weren't you asleep?)

Another way of creating hope is by using the word for hope, ummiid.
ummiid he keh tum so rahay nahi thay. (hopefully, you weren't sleeping).
This, however, is a statement and not a question.

Declension:

meñ saara din jaagta huuñ. I all day awake am.
tum saari raat jaagti ho. You all night awake are. (speaking to a woman).
ham jaagtay heñ. We awake are.
jaago! wake up!
jaagayñ! wake up! (polite)

Learn Urdu
19 March 2012 ·

Adjective of the day: gol - round.

Usage: chaand aasmaan mayñ gol nazar aa raha tha.
Trans: The moon appeared round in the sky.
Literally: moon sky in round look come ing was.

Exercises:

Fill in the blanks by answering in the comments below. Use one of the words in brackets.

vo jaag ____ (raha/rahi) thi. (he is awake)
vo jaag ____ (saktay/sakta) thay. (they could sleep)
ham ___ (sona/sota) chahtay heñ. (we want to sleep)

Learn Urdu
20 March 2012 ·

Verb of the day: nikalna - to get out

Usage: botal mayñ say paani nikal raha nahi he. jamm gaya he.
Trans: Water isn't coming out of the bottle. It has frozen.
Literally: bottle in from water get-out ing not is. frozen went is.
(As a man)

Usage: meñ pohnchnay vali huuñ. nikal ao.
Trans: I have almost reached there. Come out.
Literally: I reaching one am. get-out come.
(As a woman)

Grammar:

______ mayñ say _____

This literally means 'in from' and can be translated to 'from within' - from within the bottle.

______ jamm jaana ______

This means 'to become frozen'.
paani jamm raha he. water is in the process of freezing.
paani jamm gaya he. water has frozen.
paani sifar degree par jammta he. water freezes at zero degrees.
(sifar - zero)

______ vala ______

'vala' is an important post-position in Urdu. When it comes after a verb, like pohnchna, it translates to 'one who is about to experience the verb'. The verb, of course, goes in the prepositional case, from pohnchna to pohnchnay. vala is masculine, vali feminine and valay plural.

- pohnchnay vala - one who is about to reach
- jaanay vala - one who is about to go (masculine)
meñ jaanay vala huuñ means 'I am about to leave'.
- kehnay vali - one who is about to say (feminine)
meñ kuchh kehnay vali thi means 'I was about to say something' (as a woman)
- nikalnay valay - ones who are about to get out/leave.
ham nikalnay valay heñ means 'We are about to leave'.
- sonay vala - one who is about to sleep.
tum sonay valay/vali ho? means 'Are you about to sleep' (m/f)

'vala' can also be put infront of nouns, and here it's function changes slightly. Here 'vala' roughly translates to 'man', like milkman would be duudh-vala (duudh is milk).

- kabaaR vala means 'junk man'.
- benD valay means 'ones who play in a band'

It can be used in a wide variety of places.

Try to come up with sentences using 'vala' infront of verbs and nouns both. I will correct any mistakes.

Learn Urdu
21 March 2012 ·

Verb of the day: uchalna - to jump

Usage: vo xushi sé uchal rahi thi.
Trans: She was jumping with joy.
Literally: she joy from jump ing was.

Pronunciation change: From now on, I will use 'x' for strong 'kh', pronounced like the 'ch' in Scottish Loch or 'ch' in German 'doch'. I'm also changing 'ay' to 'é'. 'c' will be pronounced like 'ch' in church, and 'ch' will be the aspirated phoneme, pronounced like the 'ch-h' in 'touch-him'.

Grammar:

In Urdu, the verb that acts on the subject of a sentence usually has an alternative verb that acts on the object of the sentence.

uchalna is to jump and uchaalna is 'to make someone/something jump'.
Usage: us né hava méñ sikka uchaala.
Trans: he/she (transitive marker né) air in coin made-to-jump.

uchalna acts on the subject of the sentence, like 'vo' in the first example. uchaalna acts on the object of the sentence, like 'sikka' (coin) in the second example.

There are several such verb pairs in Urdu:
siikhna (to learn) - sikhaana (to teach)
bolna (to speak) - bolvaana (to make someone speak)
hilna (to move) - hilaana (to make something move)
haTna (to move aside) - haTaana (to move something aside)
jammna (to freeze) - jamaana (to make something freeze)
sona (to sleep) - solaana (to make someone fall asleep)
karna (to do) - karaana (to make someone do)

So, essentially, we're adding either 'aa', 'laa' or 'vaa' in the middle of the subject verb to get the object verb.

Usage: xud bhi kuch kaam karo awr us sé bhi kaam karaao.
Trans: Do some work yourself and make him/her work as well.
Literally: self also some work do and him/her from also work make-(him/her)-do.

Exercise:
Try to guess the first form of these verbs and write answers in the comments below!
Example: bhagaana - to make someone run. ___ bhaagna (to run)

khilaana - to make someone eat.
jagaana - to make someone wake up.
uThaana - to pick someone/something up.

nikaalna - to send someone/something out.
behkaana - to make someone go astray.
DhunDvaana - to make someone search.
rolaana - to make someone cry
hansaana - to make someone laugh

Learn Urdu
22 March 2012 ·

Word of the day: baal - hair

Usage: natasha ké baal bohot ghané heñ.
Translation: Natasha's hair are very dense.
Literally: natasha 's (of) hair very dense are.

Usage: us ké baaloñ méñ sé xushbu aa rahi he.
Trans: A nice scent ensues from here hair.
Literally: her/his of hair in from aroma come ing is.

Note: The plural of baal is also baal. The plural post-positional case is baaloñ. ghana means dense (ghana jangal - dense jungle). baal in the first sentence is plural, describing all her hair, so 'ghané' (plural of adjective ghana) is used.

Grammar:
- us ka means 'his or her', literally 'of-his or of-her', used if the noun following it is masculine. us ka khaana - her/his food.
- us ki is used if the noun after it is feminine. us ki roTi - her/his bread.
- us ké is used if the noun after it is plural. us ké baal -his/her hair.

Learn Urdu
23 March 2012 ·

Verb of the day: Darna - to fear. ڈرنا

Usage: meñ unchaaioñ sé Darta huñ.
Nastalik: میں اونچائیوں سے ڈرتا ہوں
Trans: I'm afraid of heights.
Literally: I heights from fear am.
Ru translit: мэ унчаё сей дарта ху.

Usage: us ko Dar tha, ké vo gir jaaé ga.
Nastalik: اس کو ڈر تھا کہ وہ گر جائے گا
Trans: He was afraid that he would fall.
Literally: him to fear was, that he fall go will.
(to him was fear, that he will go fall)
Ru translit: ус ко дар та, кей во гер джаэ га.

Grammar Notes:

- Dar is the noun 'fear', whereas Darna is the infinitive 'to fear' or 'to be afraid'.
- unchaa mean high. unchaai is highness or height. unchaaioñ is the post-positional case used before any post-position particle.

Learn Urdu
24 March 2012 ·

Verb of the day: Duub marna - to drown to death

Usage: kal tarbela jhiil méñ paanch tehraak Duub maré.
Urdu: کل تربیلا جھیل میں پانچ تیراک ڈوب مرے۔
Trans: Yesterday, five swimmers drowned to death in Tarbela lake.
Literal: yesterday tarbela lake in five swimmers drown died.
Ru translit: кал тарбела жил мей панч техрак дуб маре.

Grammar:
- Duubna is the infinitive 'to drown'. Duub marna is a compound verb meaning 'to drown to death'.
- tehraak is derived from the verb teherna, which means 'to swim'. tehraak is singular as well as plural

Expression:
- chullu bhar paani méñ Duub marna.
to drown to death in 'chullu' filled water.
chullu filled water in drown to-die.

- chullu is the state of the palm of one's hand which is made to hold a small amount of water, like when one tries to drink water using ones palm. The expression 'chullu bhar paani méñ Duub maro!' means 'drown to death with shame in a hand full of water!', or 'be ashamed!'

Learn Urdu
24 March 2012 ·

Word of the day: béchaara - poor (as in helpless)

Usage: vo béchaara kya kar sakta he? andha he vo.
Trans: What can that poor guy do? He's blind.
Literally: he helpless what do can is? blind is he.
Urdu: وہ بیچارہ کیا کر سکتا ہے؟ اندھا ہے وہ۔
Ru Translit: во бейчара кя кар сакта хэ? анда хэ во.

Vocabulary: Question words.

kya - کیا - кя - what
kon - کون - кон - who
kyuñ - کیوں - кю - why
kidhar - کدھر - кедэр - where
kahañ - کہاں - каха - where
kesé - کیسے - кэсей - how
kab - کب - каб - when

Learn Urdu
24 March 2012 ·

Slang of the day: jahaaz - (person) high/unaware of surroundings. (Lit. Ship)

Usage: us sé mat puucho! vo jahaaz banda he.
Urdu: اس سے مت پوچھو! وہ جہاز بندہ ہے۔
Trans: Don't ask him! He's totally high. (he's totally unaware of what's going on).
Literal: him from don't ask! he ship person is.
Ru translit: ус сей мат пучо! во жахаз банда хэ.

Usage: kya jahaaz ho tum?!
Urdu: کیا جہاز ہو تم؟!
Trans: You're so useless!
Literal: what (kind of) ship are you?!
Ru translit: кя жахаз хо тум?!

Learn Urdu
25 March 2012 ·

Verb of the day: ghabraana - to become unsettled or to fret.

Usage: mat ghabraao! sab Thiik ho jaaé ga.
Urdu: گھبراؤ مت! سب ٹھیک ہو جائے گا۔
Trans: Don't fret! Everything will be fine.
Literal: don't fret! everything fine happen go will.
Ru translit: мат габрао. саб тъик хо джае га.

Usage: vo magarmach ko dékh kar ghabraa gaya.
Urdu: وہ مگرمچ کو دیکھ کر گھبرا گیا۔
Trans: He became unsettled by looking at the crocodile.
Literal: he crocodile to see by unsettle went.
Ru translit: во магармач ко дейк кар габра гая.

Learn Urdu
25 March 2012 ·

Euphemism of the day: sar khaana - to annoy (lit. to eat someone's head).

Usage: vo bol bol kar méra sar khaa raha tha.
Urdu: وہ بول بول کر میرا سر کھا رہا تھا
Trans: He kept talking and talking and that annoyed me.
Literal: he talk talk by my head eat ing was.
Ru translit: во бол бол кар мейра сар каа раха та.

Note: kar written twice makes the action of 'doing' more pronounced

Learn Urdu
26 March 2012 ·

Word of the day: ghar - house.

Usage: mera ghar pakistan méñ he.
Urdu: میرا گھر پاکستان میں ہے
Hindi: मेरा घर पाकिस्तान में है
Trans: My house is in Pakistan.
Literal: my house pakistan in is.
Ru translit: мейра гар пакистан мей хэ.

Learn Urdu
27 March 2012 ·

Word of the day: zabaan - language or tongue. زبان

Usage: tum kitni zabaanéñ bolté ho?
Urdu: تم کتنی زبانیں بولتے ہو؟
Hindi: तुम कित्नी ज़बानें (भाषाएँ) बोल्ते हो?
Trans: How many languages do you speak?
Literal: you how-many languages speak are?
Ru translit: тум кетни забаней больте хо?

Usage: mujhé tiin zabaanéñ aati heñ.
Urdu: مجھے تین زبانیں آتی ہیں.
Hindi: मुझे तीन ज़बानें (भाषाएँ) आती हैं.
Trans: I know (how to speak) three languages.
Literal: to-me three languages come are.
Ru translit: мужей тин джабаней ати хэ.

Grammar Notes:

- kitna means 'how much' in the singular (kitna/kitni) and 'how many' in the plural forms (kitne/kitnoñ). 'kitni dawlat' (how much wealth), 'kitna pesa' (how much money), 'kitne hiiré' (how many diamonds) and 'kitnoñ ké paas he?' (how many have it?)

- The plural of zabaan is zabaanéñ. The post-positional case of the plural is zabaanoñ, which is used before the various Urdu post-positions, such as 'méñ' (in), 'ka' (of), 'sé' (from) etc.

- bolna is the verb 'to speak'.

- 'mujhé' is the pronoun 'méñ' in the dative case, which means 'to me'. It's the same as the Russian мне. 'aana' is the verb 'to come'. We use the expression 'mujhé aata/aati he' for 'I know how to'. Below is a table of dative pronouns with 'aata/aati he'. Note also that the gender of 'aata/aati he' depends on the subject of the sentence and not the dative case pronoun. In the above example, zabaan or zabaanéñ is a feminine noun. So we used 'aati heñ' for it. Also note that with an infinitive as the subject, we always use the masculine 'aata', because infinitives are all masculine.

mujhé khaana aata he. I know how to eat.
tumhé Urdu aati he. You know Urdu.
usé (or 'us ko') pakaana aata he. He/she knows how to cook. (dative of 'vo')

isé (or 'is ko') kaam aata he. He/she know how to work. (dative of 'yé')
haméñ aata/aati he. We know how to.
aap ko aata/aati he. You know how to.
un ko aata/aati he. They know (dative of vo [pl], not next to the speaker)
in ko aata/aati he. They know (dative of ye [pl], next to the speaker)

- Finally, a very useful and commonly used expression is 'mujhé pata he!' which means 'I know!' (lit. to-me address is). The dative pronouns are the same as above. 'tumhé pata he!', 'haméñ pata he!' etc. You cannot add infinitives to this expression. You can, however, add like 'mujhé us-ké baaré-méñ pata he.' 'I know about him' (lit. to-me him about address is).

Learn Urdu
28 March 2012 ·

Word of the day: dost - friend.

Usage: vo baRé saaloñ sé méra dost he.
Urdu: وہ بڑے سالوں سے میرا دوست ہے
Hind: वो बड़े सालों से मेरा दोस्त है.
Trans: He has been my friend for many years.
Literal: he big years from my friend is.

Grammar Notes:

- baRa is the adjective 'big'. It's feminine form is 'baRi' and plural is 'baRé'. Since 'years' is plural, we used 'baRé' here.

- saal means 'year'. It's plural is also 'saal' (kitné saal - how many years). saaloñ is in the post-position case, meaning it is followed by a post-position particle, like 'sé' (from) in the above usage. 'tumhari kya umar he?' (what is your age?). 'meri umar biis saal he.' (my age is twenty years).

- méra (my) is the possessive pronoun of 'meñ' (I). Below is a list of all the possessive pronouns in Urdu.

méra ______ my (m.) (méra ghar - my house)
méri _______ my (f.) (méri aavaaz - my voice)
méré ______ my (pl.) (méré haath - my hands)
tumhara _____ your (m.) (tumhara sar - your head)
tumhari _____ your (f.) (tumhari dua - your supplication)
tumharé _____ your (pl.) (tumharé haath - your hands)
us ka _______ his (us ka sar - his head)
us ki ________ her (us ki dua - her supplication)
us ké _______ his/her with a plural object. (us ké haath - his/her hands)
hamara _____ our (m.) (hamara ghar - our house)
hamari ______ our (f.) (hamari ortéñ - our women)
hamaré _____ our (pl.) (hamaré haath - our hands)
ap ka _______ your (m. pl./formal) (ap ka sar - your head)
ap ki ________ your (f. pl./formal) (ap ki dua - your supplication)
ap ké ________ your (pl./formal) (ap ké bachché - your children)
un ka ________ their (m.) or his (polite) (un ka ghar - their house / his house)
un ki ________ their (f.) or her (polite) (un ki tasveer - their picture / her picture)
un ké ________ their (pl.) or his/her (polite) (un ké haath - their hands / his|her hands)

Note that the form (a/i/é) to use depends on the gender or number of the object. 'sar' is masculine, so we use 'tumhara sar' (your head), whether speaking about a man or a woman. 'dua' is feminine, so we use 'tumhari dua' (your supplication), whether the person spoken to is a man or a woman. 'tumharé' is plural, so we say 'tumharé haath' (your hands), whether speaking to a man or a woman.

Learn Urdu
29 March 2012 ·

Word of the day: dushman - enemy

Usage: tum méré dushman ho. dafa ho!
Urdu: تم میرے دشمن ہو۔ دفع ہو!
Hindi: तुम मेरे दुश्मन हो. दफा हो!
Trans: You're my enemy. Get lost!
Literal: you my enemy are. gone be!

Grammar notes:

'ho!' is the imperative form of hona (to be). The informal imperative is formed simply by removing the 'na' ending of the infinitive and adding an 'o' at the end.
karna - karo! do!
jaagna - jaago! wake up!

Learn Urdu
30 March 2012 ·

an alternative way to express:
دیکھنا
देखना
dekhnaa = to see

it can sometimes give the sense that the looking was not voluntary or intentional.
کو نظر آنا
को नज़र आना
ko nazar (F) aanaa = sight to come to.
the subject seeing takes a KO, always. although nazar is feminine, the aanaa will take on the gender form of whatever the subject is regarding. for example:

मुझे नज़र आ रहा है कि आप को मज़ा आया
mujhe nazar aa rahaa hai ki aap ko mazaa aaya = LIT: me to sight coming is that you to fun came = i am seeing that you had fun
the aa rahaa here is in the masculine because they are discussing the 'mazaa' (fun) and mazaa is masculine

another example:
!مجھے بہت مٹھایاں نظر آتی ہیں
मुझे बहुत मिठाइयाँ नज़र आती हैं
mujhe bahut miTHaaiyaan nazar aati hain = i see a lot of sweets!

Note: There is no 'KO' (to) after mujhe (to me) because 'mujhe' incorporates a 'to' within it. Another way of saying 'mujhe' is 'mujh ko'. Similarly, 'tumhe' can also be 'tum ko' and 'use/ise' can be 'usko/isko'. haméñ can be 'ham ko' and 'unhéñ/inhéñ' can be 'unko/inko'. Nice post, John.

Learn Urdu
31 March 2012 ·

Word of the day: ghuurna - to stare.

Usage: vo shaam ké vakt chodhviiñ ké chaand ki taraf ghuur raha tha.
Urdu: وہ شام کے وقت چودھویں کے چاند کی طرف گھور رہا تھا.
Trans: He was staring at the full moon in the evening.
Literally: he evening of time fourteenth of moon towards stare ing was.

Grammar notes:

- taraf means direction or side. chaand ki taraf means 'in the direction of the moon' or 'towards the moon'. taraf is feminine, 'meri taraf' (towards me), 'tumhari taraf' (towards you), so the possessive pronoun before it always has to be feminine. 'ki' (of) is also in the feminine form because of this reason.

- we use 'chodhviiñ ka chaand' to denote the 'full moon'. It literally means the moon of the fourteenth (night).

Learn Urdu
1 April 2012 ·

Word of the day: acha lagna (alternates achi lagna/ache lagna) to like, lit. to seem good.

Usage: mujhe Fahd acha seem he.
Urdu: مجھے فہد اچھا لگتا ہے
Trans: I like Fahd.
Literal: to-me Fahe good hits is.
Ру Буквы: муже фахд ача лагта хэ.

Usage: saari dunya ko meñ achi lagti huñ.
Urdu: ساری دنیا کو میں اچھی لگتی ہوں
Trans: The world likes me. (meñ is a woman in this sentence, so 'lagti')
Literal: all world to I good seem am.
Ру буквы: сари дуня ко мэ ачи лагти ху.

Usage: tumhé baccé aché lagté heñ.
Urdu: تمھے بچے اچھے لگتے ہیں
Trans: You like children.
Literal: to-you children good seem are.
Ру буквы: тумхе баччей ачей лагтей хэ.

Grammar notes:

- lagna literally means 'to be hit'. However, it is mostly used to mean 'to seem'. 'mujhe lagta he' means 'it seems to me' (lit. to-me seems is). 'mujhe lagta he, keh vo Dar raha he' means 'it seems to me that he is scared'. In this case, we always use 'lagta' irrespective of personal pronoun, 'meñ' or 'tum' or 'vo'. In the above examples though, it agrees with gender and number (lagta/lagti/lagte). 'meñ' was a woman in the second example, so we used 'lagti'. 'Fahd' is a boy, so we used 'lagta'. 'baccé' is plural, so we use 'lagté' to agree with it's plurality.

Learn Urdu
2 April 2012 ·

Word of the day: laRna - to fight.

Usage: gali méñ do ghunDé apas méñ laR rahé thé.
Trans: Two thugs were fighting each other in the street.
Literal: street in two thugs themselves in fight ing were.

Grammar notes:

- apas méñ means 'among themselves' or 'among ourselves' depending on the context.

Learn Urdu
3 April 2012 ·

Word of the day: pasand hona - to like

Usage: mujhe shatranj khélna pasand he.
Trans: I like to play chess.
Literal: to-me chess to-play liked is.

Usage: mujhe tum pasand ho.
Trans: I like you. or I am fond of you.
Literal: to-me you liked are.

Learn Urdu
5 April 2012 ·

Word of the day: galé milna - to hug (lit. to meet necks)

Usage: vo galé mil rahe heñ.
Urdu: وہ گلے مل رہے ہیں
Trans: They are hugging.
Literal: they necks meet ing are.
Ru: во галей мел рахе хе.

Learn Urdu
9 April 2012 ·

Word of the day: us ké baad - after that

Usage: meñ pehlé ghar jaauñ ga (jaauñ gi). us ké baad mujhé bahir jaana he.
Trans: I will go home first. After that, I want to go out.
Literal: I first home go will. That of after to-me outside to-go is.

Grammar notes:

- 'mujhé infinitive he' or 'tumhé infinitive he' are forms that are used to mean 'I want to infinitive' or 'you want to infinitive'.
'mujhé kuch khaana he' means 'I want to eat something'. It is an indirect way of saying that you want something, instead of 'meñ kuch khaana chahta/chahti huñ'.

Learn Urdu
15 April 2012 ·

Word of the day: hava - air, wind.

Usage: aj bohot téz hava chal rahi he.
Trans: A very strong wind is blowing today.
Literal: today very fast wind walk ing is.

Learn Urdu
1 May 2012 ·

Word of the day: sabzi - vegetable

Usage: tum aj konsi sabzi khao gi?
Trans: Which vegetable will you eat today?
Literally: You today which vegetable eat will?

Grammar notes:

- konsa/konsi/konsé mean 'which'. 'konsa ghar' - which house. 'konsi gaaRi' - which car. 'konsé laRké' - which boys.
- khao ge/khao gi is the future tense of khate ho/khati ho. In the future tense, we only use 'ga/ge' for masculine and 'gi' for feminine. The verb changes form according to the person using it.

meN khauN ga/gi - I (m/f) will eat.
tum khao ge/gi - you (m/f) will eat.
vo khae ga/gi - he/she will eat.
ham khaeN ge - we will eat.
vo khaeN ge - they will eat.
ap khaeN ge - you (pl/for) will eat.

Learn Urdu
7 May 2012 ·

Word of the day: bakwaas - nonsense (bullshit)

Usage: sayasatdaan aj kal sirf bakwaas karte rehte hen.
Trans: Nowadays, politicians keep on uttering nonsense.
Literally: politicians now-adays only bullshit do stay are.

Grammar notes:
'rehna' literally means 'to stay' or 'to reside (somewhere).'
karte rehna is a compound infinitive that means 'to keep on doing'.
hote rehna means 'to keep on happening'.
bolte rehna means 'to keep on speaking/talking'
chalte rehna means 'to keep on walking'

You catch my drift.

It conjugates like normal verbs.
men sara din sota rehta hun - I keep on sleeping all (sara) day (din). [as a man]
men sara din soti rehti hun - I keep on sleeping all day.
ham sara din sote rehte hen - We keep on sleeping all day.
men sara din sote-rehna chahta hun - I want to keep on sleeping all day.

From the last sentence, you see that the compound infinitive has 'sote' instead of 'sota' or 'soti' as a rule. In the last sentence, 'sote rehna' is the second verb (infinitive) and 'chahta' is the first verb (present tense).

Learn Urdu
15 May 2012 ·

Word of the day: tang karna - to irritate

Usage: mujhe tang na karo!
Trans: Don't irritate me!
Literal: to-me narrow not do!

Note: 'tang' itself means narrow, like a narrow alley (tang gali).

Learn Urdu
20 May 2012 ·

Word of the day: thappaR - slap

Usage: us né usé thappaR maara.
Trans: He slapped him.
Literal: He (né) him slap hit.

Notes:
This sentence can also be translated to 'He slapped her' or 'She slapped her' or 'She slapped him'. Depends on the context.
'maarna' means 'to beat' or 'to hit'. 'thappaR' is a noun only, unlike the English 'slap', which is both a noun and a verb. 'thappaR maarna' is the compound verb that means 'to slap'.

Learn Urdu
23 May 2012 ·

Word of the day: chahié - want (for nouns)

We have seen before how to say "I want to drink" (meN khaana chahta/i huN) or "I want <insert verb>". To say, "I want an apple" or "I want <insert noun>," we need 'chahié'. It always goes with the dative case (to- case) of the pronoun (mujhé, tumhé, usé, haméN, apko, unhé)

Usage: mujhé ék séb chahié he.
Trans: I want an apple.
Literal: to-me an apple wanted is.
Urdu: مجھے ایک سیب چاہئے.

Usage: tumhé kuchh chahié tha?
Trans: Did you want something?
Literal: to-you something wanted was?
Urdu: تجھے کچھ چاہئے تھا؟

Learn Urdu
24 May 2012 ·

Word of the day: sabzi - vegetable

Usage: aj khaané méñ mujhé koi sabzi chahié he.
Trans: I want some vegetable for lunch today.
Literal: today food in to-me any vegetable wanted is.

Grammar: khaané is in the post-postional case, its nominative being khaana.

Vocabulary: sabziañ - vegetables

daal - lentils
saag - spinach
gaajar - carrot
muli - radish
bhinDi - lady fingers
bhengan - brinjals
nimbu - lemon

TamaTar - tomato
dhania - coriander
pyaaz - onion
thom - garlic
adrak - ginger
podina - mint
karela - bitter gourd
kaddu - bottle gourd
khiira - cucumber
ziira - cumin
hari mirch - green chilly
laal mirch - red chilly
shimla mirch - green pepper (or any colour)
aalu - potato

Learn Urdu
25 May 2012 ·

Vocabulary of the day: phal - fruit

séb - apple
malTa - orange
kéla - banana
anaar - pomegranate
angur - grapes
nashpaati - pear
aam - manga
chakotra - grape fruit
amruud - guava
tarbuuz - water melon
xarbuuza - melon
garma - musk melon
papiita - papaya
shehtuut - berry
xubaani - apricot
bér - jujube fruit

Learn Urdu
1 June 2012 ·

Word of the day: chhuri - knife

Usage: mujhé séb kaatné ké lié chhuri chahié he.
Translation: I need a knife to cut an apple.
Literally: to-me apple to-cut for knife wanted is.
Urdu: مجھے سیب کاٹنے کے لیے چھری چاہیے ہے

Vocabulary: Kitchen - bavarchi xana

chamach - spoon
kaanTa - fork
pléT/thaali - plate
pyaali - cup
Tré/ghori - tray
chuulha - stove
aag - fire
avan - oven
nalka - tap
chiini - sugar
namak - salt
pani - water
duudh - milk

Learn Urdu
17 June 2012 ·

Word of the day: shaxsīat (fem) - personality

Usage: us ki shaxsīat ki lōg tārīf karté heṇ.
Trans: People praise his personality.
Literal: his-of personality-of people praise do are.

Note: shaxsīat comes from the word 'shaxs', which means person. 'x' is pronounced like the 'ch' in German 'doch'.

Learn Urdu
19 June 2012 ·

Word of the day: lālach - greed

Usage: lālach buri balā he.
Trans: Greed is a curse.
Literal: greed bad monster is.

Learn Urdu
20 June 2012 ·

Word of the day: samundar (m) - sea

Usage: meṇ samundar méṇ teherné gaya tha/gai thi.
Trans: I went for a swim in the sea.
Literal: I sea in to-swim went was.

Usage: iss samundar méṇ teherna xatarnāk he.
Trans: swimming in this sea is dangerous.
Literal: this sea in to-swim dangerous is.

Origin: Sanskrit - Samudra (lit. 'gather of waters'. sam means 'together' in Sanskrit and udra means 'water'.)

Facts: 'Together' can be translated to 'sammen' in Norwegian and Danish, 'samen' in Icelandic and Dutch, 'insieme' in Italian, 'zusammen' in German, 'ensemble' in French, 'simul' in Latin (from which we get 'simultaneously'), and sama in Bahasa and Tagalog. All these languages have the root 'sam' or 's-m' in them. It shows their proximity to Sanskrit.

Vocabulary: Water - pāni

daryā (m) - river
neher/nadi (f) - stream
jhīl (f) - lake
kuṇwa (m) - well

Learn Urdu
24 June 2012 ·

Word of the day: mukka - punch

Usage: Ibrahim né Abdul ké muuṇ par mukka maara.
Translation: Ibrahim blew a punch on Abdul's face.
Literally: Ibrahim (erg) Abdul-of mouth-on punch hit.

Grammar notes:

- maarna means 'to hit/to beat'. maara is the simple past tense of maarna. Since 'maara' takes an object, (being a transitive verb) the subject (Ibrahim in this case) has to be followed by the 'né' post-position. This feature of distinguishing between transitive and intransitive verbs is called ergativity; the language possessive an 'ergative case'.

- In Urdu-Hindi, we don't punch or slap someone's face - we punch or slap someone's mouth.

PS: No Abdul was harmed in the making of this post.

Learn Urdu
25 June 2012 ·

Word of the day: machhar - mosquito

Usage: ék machhar mujhé ungli par kāT raha he.
Translation: A mosquito is biting my finger.
Literally: one mosquito to-me finger-on cut-ing is.

Vocabulary: Insects - kīRé

makkhi - fly
shehd ki makkhi - bee (lit. honey fly)
chūnTi - ant
khaTmal - cockroach

Grammar notes: kāTna - to cut

Urdu is one of the few languages that can match English tenses and add certain moods and aspects onto them.

meṇ kāTta hun - I cut. (present tense)
meṇ kāT raha hun - I am cutting. (present continuous)
meṇ kāT chuka hun - I have cut (just finished) (present perfect)
meṇ né kāTa hua he - I have cut (already) (present perfect)
meṇ né kāT lia he - I have cut (for myself).
meṇ né kāT dia he - I have cut (for you/him/her)
meṇ kāTne vala huṇ - I am about to cut.
meṇ kāTta rehta huṇ - I keep cutting.

meṇ né kāTa - I cut. (simple past)
meṇ né kāTa tha - I cut. (past tense)
meṇ kāT raha tha - I was cutting (past continuous)
meṇ né kāTa hua tha - I had cut (already) (past perfect)
meṇ kāT chuka tha - I had cut (just finished) (past perfect)
meṇ né kāT lia tha - I had cut (for myself)
meṇ né kāT dia tha - I had cut (for you/him/her)
meṇ kāTné vala tha - I was about to cut.
meṇ kāTta tha - I used to cut.
meṇ kāTta rehta tha - I used to keep on cutting.
meṇ kāTta raha - I kept on cutting.
meṇ né kāTa hua ho ga - I must have cut it.

meṇ kāTuṇ ga - I will cut (future tense)
meṇ kāT raha huṇ ga - I will be cutting (future continuous)
meṇ kāTné vala huṇ - I am about to cut.
meṇ kāTné vala huṇ ga - I will be about to cut.
meṇ kāT chuka huṇ ga - I will have cut.
meṇ kāT luṇ ga - I will cut (for myself)
meṇ kāT duṇ ga - I will cut (for you/him/her/someone)
meṇ kāTta rahuṇ ga - I will keep on cutting.

There are other possibilities I've left out. Also, all the subjects and objects in these sentences are masculine. We can make three more sets of sentences like this one by adding a masculine subject feminine object, feminine subject masculine object, and feminine subject feminine object.

Learn Urdu
29 June 2012 ·

Word of the day: esh-o-ishrat - luxury

Usage: Hannan Canada méṇ esh-o-ishrat ki zindagi guzār raha he.
Translation: Hannan is living a life of luxury in Canada.
Literally: Hannan Canada-in luxury of life spend-ing is.

Grammar Notes: guzārna - to spend (time)

meṇ guzārta huṇ - I spend (time). (masc)
meṇ guzārti huṇ - I spend (time). (fem)
meṇ vakt guzār raha huṇ - I am spending time. (masc)

tum vakt guzār rahi thi - You were spending time. (fem)
vo Pakistan méṇ vakt guzār chuki he - She has spent time in Pakistan.
us né ked-xané méṇ vakt guzāra he - He/She has spent time in jail.

ham vahāṇ vakt guzārna chahté heṇ - We want to spend time there.
kya vo yahāṇ vakt guzār sakté heṇ? - Can they spend time here?

Learn Urdu
1 July 2012 ·

Word of the day: daftar - office.

Usage: meṇ daftar méṇ beTha huṇ.
Translation: I am sitting at the office.
Literally: I office-in seated am.

Learn Urdu
10 July 2012 ·

Word of the day: bīmār (adj.) - ill, sick.

Usage: Hannan bīmār rehta he aj kal.
Translation: Hannan stays sick these days.
Literally: Hannan ill stays is nowadays.

Vocabulary:

bīmāri (noun) - illness
bīmāriaṇ (plural)
bīmārioṇ (oblique plural - used with post-positions)

Usage: tumhē kyā bīmāri he?
Trans: What is your problem?
Literal: to-you what ilness is?

Usage: bīmāriaṇ aam ho gai heṇ.
Trans: Illnesses have grown commonplace.
Literal: illnesses common become gone are.

Usage: in bīmārioṇ ka kya ilāj he?
Trans: What is the cure for these illnesses?
Literal: these illnesses of what cure is?

Learn Urdu
12 July 2012 ·

Word of the day: zilzila - earthquake.

Usage: aj pakistan me zilzila aaya.
Translation: there was an earthquake in Pakistan today.
Literally: today pakistan-in earthquake came.

Verb: aana - to come.

me aata hu - I come.
me aaya tha - I came. (men)
me aai thi - I came. (women)
me aaun ga - I will come. (men)
me aaun gi - I will come. (women)

Learn Urdu
19 July 2012 ·

Word of the day: habs - humidity

Usage: aj bohot habs he.
Translation: It's very humid today.
Literally: today very humid is.

Learn Urdu
6 August 2012 ·

Word of the day: nayāb - rare, exotic.

Usage: meṇ né hāl hi méṇ ék nayāb hīrā xarīda he.
Translation: I have recently bought a rare diamond.
Literally: I (né) recently one rare diamond bought.

Notes:

hāl hi méṇ - recently. (in the recent present)
meṇ né xarīda - I bought (simple past)
meṇ né xarīda he - I have bought.
meṇ né xarīda tha - I had bought.

Learn Urdu
27 August 2012 ·

Word of the day: saka - could (simple past of sakna)

Usage: men vakt par pohonch na saka/saki.
Translation: I could not reach on time.
Literally: I time on reach not could.
Urdu: میں وقت پہ پہنچ نہ سکا-

Learn Urdu
11 September 2012 ·

Word of the day: mor - peacock.

Usage: ye ek mor he.
Translation: this is a peacock.
Literally: this a peacock is.

Learn Urdu
12 September 2012 ·

Word of the day: moTa - fat

Usage: men moTa nahi hun. bas meri haDDian bhaari hen.
Translation: I'm not fat. I'm just big boned.
Literally: I fat not am. just my bones heavy are.

Notes:
- moTa (masc), moTi (femn), moTe (plur)
- haDDi (bone - feminine noun), haDDian (bones)
- meri (my - for femn.), mera (my - for masc.), mere (my - for plural)
- bas (just)
- bhaar (weight - noun), bhaari (heavy - adj.)

Learn Urdu
14 September 2012 ·

Word of the day: aandhi - storm.

Usage: shadiid aandhi chal rahi he baahir.
Translation: There's a strong storm outside.
Literally: extreme storm walk ing is outside.

Learn Urdu
21 September 2012 ·

Word of the day: gaana - to sing (v.), song (n.)

Usage: Ibraheem gaana gaate hue gir gaya.
Translation: Ibraheem fell down while singing a song.
Literally: Ibraheem song singing-while fell went.

Notes:
girna - to fall
gir jaana - to fall down.
gir gaya/gir gai - fell down (m./f.)

hue is used here as 'while'.
gaate hue - while singing.
jaate hue - while going.
aate hue - while coming.
khaate hue - while eating.
bolte hue - while speaking.

Learn Urdu
11 October 2012 ·

Word of the day: bhuulna - to forget

Usage: baarish ho rahi he, or men apni chhatri ghar bhuul aaya huun. (boy speaking)
Usage: baarish ho rahi he, or men apni chhatri ghar bhuul aai huun. (girl speaking)
Translation: It is raining, and I forgot my umbrella at home.
Literally: rain happen-ing is, and I my umbrella home forget came am.

Note:
We are obliged to mention whether we have 'come' somewhere (bhuul aaya) after forgetting the object, or 'went' somewhere (bhuul gaya).

baarish - rain
ho raha hona - to be happening
or - and
chhatri - umbrella
bhuul aana - to forget (saying that you forgot something after arriving somewhere)

Learn Urdu
13 October 2012 ·

Word of ze day: vehshi - wild

Usage: yahan log vehshi jaanvaron ki tarah hen.
Translation: The people here are like wild animals.
Literally: here people wild animals of type are.

Usage: vehshi, yaar!!
Translation: awesome, man!!
Literally: awesome, friend!!

Learn Urdu
15 October 2012 ·

Word of the day: thiiTa - nerd

Usage: yar, us thiiTe se puucho is savaal ka javaab.
Translation: man, ask that nerd the answer to this question.
Literally: man, that nerd from ask this question of answer.

Learn Urdu
16 October 2012 ·

Word of the day: rang - colour

Usage: meri kamiz ka rang niila he.
Translation: My shirt's colour is blue.
Literally: my shirt of colour blue is.

Colours - rang

niila/niili - blue (m/f)
kaala/kaali - black (m/f)
laal or surkh - red (gender-free)
safed - white
hara/hari - green (m/f)
zard - yellow
piaazi - pink
saleTi - grey
naranji - orange
ferozi - light blue

Learn Urdu
26 October 2012 ·

Word of the day: mehsuus karna - to feel

Usage: men aj acha mehsus kar raha hun
Translation: I'm feeling good today.
Literally: I today good feel do ing am.

Learn Urdu
9 November 2012 ·

Word of the day: intehaai - extremely

Usage: Ibrahim intehaai acha larka he.
Translation: Ibrahim is an extremely good boy.
Literally: Ibrahim extremely good boy is.

Learn Urdu
19 October 2012 ·

Word of the day: bhuut - ghost

Usage: ese lagta he jese tum ne bhuut dekh lia ho.
Translation: It seems as if you've seen a ghost.
Literally: like-this seems is like you ghost seen have.

Learn Urdu
10 November 2012 ·

Word of the day: fazuul kharch - spend-thrift

Usage: Amir intehaai fazuul kharch insaan he.
Translation: Amir is a real spend-thrift.
Literally: Amir extremely unnecessary spending human is.

Learn Urdu
28 December 2012 ·

Word of the day: pehla - first

Usage: yakam janvari saal ka pehla din he.
Trans: First of January is the first day of the year.
Literal: first january year of first day is.

Learn Urdu
28 December 2012 ·

Word of the day: pehla - first

Usage: yakam janvari saal ka pehla din he.
Trans: First of January is the first day of the year.
Literal: first january year of first day is.

Learn Urdu
9 March 2013 ·

Word of the day: sanbhaalna - سنبھالنا
- to take care of (sth.)
- to store (sth.)
- to put away (sth.)
- to handle (sth. or someone)

Usage: اپنے کپڑے سنبھال لو
Transliteration: apne kapRe sanbhaal lo!
Translation: Put away your clothes!
Literally: your clothes take-care lo!

Note: 'lo' (imperative) is used before a verb to indicate that the action is intended for the subject in the sentence. Same goes for 'lia' in the next example; 'lia' being the past form.

Usage: میں نے کام سنبھال لیا تھا
Transliteration: men ne kaam sanbhaal lia tha.
Translation: I had taken care of the work.
Literally: I (ne) work taken-care (lia) was.

Learn Urdu
21 March 2013 ·

Word of the day: DanDa - stick.

Usage: polees vala DanDa haath main pakRe khaRa tha.
Translation: The policeman stood holding a stick.
Literally: police one stick hand-in holding standing was.

Learn Urdu
12 April 2013 ·

Pakistan main intikhabat honay walay hain.

Pakistan in elections are about to happen.

Elections are about to happen in Pakistan.

Learn Urdu
22 April 2013 ·

Word of the day: ghubaara - balloon

Usage: ammi, mujhe ghubaara chahie he.
Translation: Mom, I want a balloon.
Literally: mom, to-me balloon wanted is

Learn Urdu
11 May 2013 ·

Word of the day: intekhabaat - elections

Usage: آج پاکستان میں انتخابات کا دن ہے.
Transliteration: aj pakistan main intekhabaat ka din he.
Translation: It's election day today in Pakistan.
Literally: today pakistan in elections of day is.

Learn Urdu
23 April 2013 ·

Word of the day: chammach - spoon

Usage: main chammach dho raha/rahi hun.
Translation: I'm washing the spoon.
Literally: I spoon wash-ing am.

Notes:
dhona - to wash
haath dhona - to wash hands
kapRe dhona - to wash clothes
bartan dhona - to wash utensils

Vocabulary:
kaanTa - fork
chhuri - knife
pyaala - bowl
pyaali - cup
thaali - plate
ghori - tray
chainak - teapot
botal - bottle
khanjar - dagger

Learn Urdu
10 May 2013 ·

Word of the day: neya (masc.) - new

Alternate forms: naii (fem.), nae (plural.)

Usage: عمران خان ایک نیا پاکستان بنانا چہتا ہے
Tranlisteration: imran khan ek naya pakistan banaana chahta he.
Translation: Imran Khan wants to create a new Pakistan.
Literally: imran khan a new pakistan to-make wants is.

Learn Urdu
2 May 2013 ·

Word of the day: bahaar - spring

Usage: مجھے بہار کا موسم اچھا لگتا ہے
Transliteration: mujhe bahaar ka mosam acha lagta he.
Translation: I like the spring season.
Literally: to-me spring of season good feels is.

Vocabulary: mosam - season/weather

bahaar - spring
xazaaN - autumn
garmiaN - summers
sardiaN - winters

Note: garmiaN and sardiaN are plurals, and they are used this way to represent the summer and winter seasons. You can also say:
'garmi ka mosam' (lit. season of heat)
'sardi ka mosam' (lit. season of cold)
'bahaar ka mosam'
'xazaaN ka mosam.'

Learn Urdu
14 May 2013 ·

Word of the day: puraana - old, archaic.

Other forms: puraani (feminine), puraane (plural)

Usage: پنجاب کو پرانا پاکستان پسند ہے
Transliteration: punjab ko puraana pakistan pasand he.
Translation: Punjab likes old Pakistan.
Literally: punjab to old pakistan liked is.

Learn Urdu
31 May 2013 ·

Word of the day: hazaar - thousand

Usage: آج اس صفحے کو ہزار سے زائد لوگوں نے پسند کیا ہے.
Translit: aj is safeh ko hazaar se zaaid logon ne pasand kia he.
Translation: Today, over a thousand people have liked this page.
Literally: today this page-to thousand-than more people (ne) liked done have.

Learn Urdu
27 June 2013 ·

Word of the day: gaana - song/to sing

Usage: آئی ٹو آئی گانا گانا ممنوع ہے
Transliteration: eye to eye gaana gaana mamnuu he.
Word-by-word: eye to eye song to-sing forbidden is.
Translation: It is forbidden to sing the song 'Eye to eye'.

Usage: میں گانا گا رہا\رہی ہوں
Tranlisteration: meN gaana gaa raha/rahi huN
Word-by-word: i song sing-ing am.
Translation: I'm singing a song.

Learn Urdu
12 July 2013 ·

Word of the day: roza (n.) - fast

Usage: رمضان میں اکثر لوگ روزہ رکھتے ہیں
Transliteration: ramzan meN aksar log roza rakhte heN
Translation: Several people fast in Ramzan.
Literally: ramzan-in several people fast keep are.

Learn Urdu
28 July 2013 ·

Word of the day: mazduri - labour/physical work

Usage: میں روزی کمانے کے لیے مزدوری کرتا ہوں-
Transliteration: meN rozi kamaane ke liye mazduuri karta huuN.
Translation: I do physical labour to earn a living.
Word by word: I a living earning for labour do am.

Note:
rozi kamaana - to make a living

Learn Urdu

30 July 2013 ·

Word of the day: dekhna - to see

Usage: میں نے ایک لڑکی دیکھی
Transliteration: meN ne ek laRki dekhi.
Translation: I saw a girl.
Literally: I (transitive particle 'ne') a girl saw.

Usage: میں نے ایک لڑکی کو دیکھا
Transliteration: meN ne ek laRki ko dekha.
Translation: I looked at a girl.
Literally: I (ne) a girl at looked.

Grammar notes:

When the verb is acting on laRki alone, it declines in gender accordingly.

When the post-position 'ko' (to/at) is added, the masculine simple past of dekhna - dekha - is always used.

Learn Urdu

23 August 2013 ·

Word of the day: gaon - village

Usage: عام طور پر گاؤں کی ہوا شہر کی ہوا سے زیادہ صاف ہوتی ہے
Transliteration: aam tor par gaon ki hava sheher ki hava se ziada saaf hoti he.
Translation: Normally, village air is cleaner than city air.
Literally: normal way on village-of air city-of air than more clean is.

Learn Urdu
25 August 2013 ·

Word of the day: tak - until

Usage: میں جب تک تھکتا\تھکتی نہیں، تب تک دوڑونگا\گی۔
Transliteration: men jab tak thakta/thakti nahi, tab tak doRun ga/gi.
Translation: I will run until I get tired.
Literally: I until when tire not, until then will-run.

Usage: تم کب تک یہاں رہو گے\گی؟
Transliteration: tum kab tak yahan raho ge/gi?
Translation: Until when are you going to stay here?
Literally: you until when here stay will?

Note: kab (when) is used as a question word. jab (when) is used to make a statement. English does not make this distinction, and uses 'when' in both cases.

Learn Urdu
26 August 2013 ·

Word of the day: barish - rain

Usage: آج بارش ہو رہی ہے۔ میں باہر نہیں جا سکتا\سکتی۔
Transliteration: aj barish ho rahi he. men bahir nahi ja sakta/sakti.
Translation: It is raining today. I cannot go out.
Literally: today rain happening is. i outside not go can.

Learn Urdu
28 August 2013 ·

Vocabulary of the day: mawsam - season, weather.

Most parts of India and Pakistan enjoy all four seasons to the max. The year starts off with a chilly winter (سردی sardi - also means cold), followed by a spring (بہار bahaar) that couldn't be more beautiful; with endless fields adorned by bright yellow flowers of the mustard crop. I find driving through these fields, smelling the true scent of spring, one of the most relaxing activities in existence. Temperatures during the spring go usually from a mild 20 up to a warm 30 degrees. The summer (گرمی garmi - also means heat) takes over with a blast of hot wind and strong sun that make one want to stay home and do nothing. Or maybe that's just me. Then autumn (خزاں khazaan) jumps in, and no matter how dull it may be, it is always welcome after the long months of sun burns and heavy sweating. And finally we get back to sardi, which takes me by surprise every single year - unprepared as I always am for the low temperatures and spine shaking breezes.

بہرحال، مختلف موسموں کی وجہ سے سال اتنا بےرنگ نہیں لگتا۔
behrhaal, mukhtalif mawsmon ki vajah se saal itna berang nahi lagta.
(anyway, different seasons of reason from year so monotonous not seems.)

Learn Urdu
30 August 2013 ·

Word of the day: sui - needle

Usage: میں کپڑے سی رہی تھی اور مجھے سوئی چبھ گئی۔
Tranliteration: men kapRe sii rahi thi or mujhe sui chubh gai.
Translation: As I was sewing clothes, I pricked myself.
Literally: I clothes sew ing was and to-me needle pricked.

Learn Urdu
30 August 2013 ·

Word of the day: bivi - wife (also begam)

Usage: وہ اپنی بیوی کے ساتھ امریکے جائے گا۔
Transliteration: vo apni bivi ke saath amrike jaaega.
Translation: He will go to the US with his wife.
Literally: he his wife with america will-go.

Learn Urdu
30 August 2013 ·

Word of the day: shohar - husband (also khaavand)

Usage: میرے شوہر کا نام ابراھیم ہے۔
Transliteration: mere shohar ka naam ibrahim he.
Translation: My husband's name is Ibrahim.
Literally: my husband of name ibrahim is.

Learn Urdu
4 September 2013 ·

Word of the day: gila (m.) - wet (gili[f.]/gile[pl.])

Usage: میرے کپڑے بارش میں گیلے ہو گئے.
Transliteration: mere kapRe barish men gile ho gae.
Transtion: My clothes got wet in the rain.
Literally: my clothes rain in wet became.

Vocabulary:

gili kamiz - wet shirt
gili shalvar - wet pajamas
gile baal - wet hair
gile haath - wet hands
gila chehra - wet face
gila matha - wet forehead

Learn Urdu
5 September 2013 ·

Word of the day: khelna - to play

Usage: میں کرکٹ کھیلنا چاہتا\چاہتی ہوں.
Transliteration: men cricket khelna chahta/chahti hun
Translation: I want to play cricket.
Literally: I cricket to-play want(m/f) am.

Learn Urdu
11 September 2013 ·

Word of the day: bekaar - useless

Usage: اتوار کے دن بازار جانا بیکار ہے۔ سب دکانیں بند ہوتی ہیں۔
Transliteration: itvaar ke din bazaar jaana bekaar he. sab dukaaneñ band hoti heñ.
Translation: It is useless to go to the market on Sundays. All the shops are closed.
Literally: sunday-of-day market to-go useless is. all shops closed are.

Vocabulary:

Days of the Week (hafta) in Urdu

piir - monday
mangal - tuesday
budh - wednesday
jumeraat - thursday (night of juma; raat - night)
juma - friday
hafta - saturday (also means 'week' itself; comes from persian haft, meaning seven)
itvaar - sunday

(mangal and budh are derived directly from hindi)

Days of the Week in Hindi

somvaar - monday
mangalvaar - tuesday
budhvaar - wednesday
guruvaar/vrihaspativaar - thursday
shukravaar - friday
shanivaar - saturday
ravivaar - sunday

Learn Urdu
11 September 2013 ·

Word of the day: sharmaana - to feel shy/abashed

Usage: شیر شیرنی کو دیکھ کر شرما گیا۔

Transliteration: sher sherni ko dekh ke sharmaa gaya.

Translation: The tiger felt shy looking at the tigress.

Literally: tiger tigress to see by shy went.

Learn Urdu
15 September 2013 ·

Word of the day: ghabraana - to feel anxious.

Usage: ایکسیڈنٹ کے بعد وہ اپنے والدین کے ساتھ بات کرتے ہوئے گھبرا رہا تھا۔

Transliteration: accident ke baad vo apne vāldēn se bāt karte hue ghabrā raha tha.

Translation: He was feeling anxious talking to his parents after the accident.

Literally: accident of after he his parents with in-the-state-of-doing-talk (bāt-karte-hue) anxious -ing (continuous tense) was.

Note: karte hue above means 'being in the state of doing' something.

vo khāna khāte hue bol rahi thi.
she food in-the-state-of-eating speak ing was.

It can also be read as 'while'. She was speaking while eating food.

Learn Urdu
22 September 2013 ·

Word of the day: phēnkna - to throw

Usage: تم وہاں کیا پھینک رہی ہو؟
Transliteration: tum vahān kyā phēnk rahi ho?
Translation: What are you throwing over there.
Literally: you there what throw-ing are?

Learn Urdu
23 September 2013 ·

Word of the day: dhona - to wash

Usage: اپنے ہاتھ دھو لو۔
Transliteration: apne haath dho lo!
Translation: Wash your hands!
Literally: your hands wash!

Learn Urdu
5 October 2013 ·

Word of the day: jhūt bolna - to lie/to tell a lie

Usage: وہ سارا وقت جھوٹ بول رہا تھا \ رہی تھی۔
Transliteration: vo sāra vakt jhūt bol raha tha / rahi thi.
Translation: He/she was lying all this time.
Literally: he/she all time lie speak ing was.

Learn Urdu
18 October 2013 ·

Word of the day: dāen - right

Usage: دائیں ہاتھ پے مڑ جاؤ یہاں۔
Transliteration: dāen hāth pe muR jao yahān.
Translation: Turn right here.
Literally: right hand on turn go here.

Learn Urdu
23 October 2013 ·

Word of the day: pēdal - on foot

Usage: میں آج دفتر پیدل جا رہا ہوں۔
Tranliteration: men āj daftar pēdal jā raha hun.
Translation: Today I'm going to work on foot.
Literally: I today work on-foot go ing am.

Learn Urdu
26 October 2013 ·

Word of the day: rāz - secret

Usage: یہ ایک بہت بڑا راز ہے.
Transliteration: ye ek bohot bara rāz he.
Translation: It is a big secret.
Literally: this a very big secret is.

Learn Urdu
1 November 2013 ·

Word of the day: daryā - river

Usage: دریائے ہند کشمیر، سرحد، پنجاب، اور سندھ کے صوبوں میں سے گزرتا ہے۔
Transliteration: daryā-e-hind kashmir, sarhad, panjab, or sindh ke sūboṇ meṇ se guzarta he.
Translation: The river Indus passes through the provinces of Kashmir, Frontier, Punjab, and Sindh.
Literally: river-of-Indus Kashmir, Frontier, Punjab, and Sindh of pronvinces in from passes is.

Note: meṇ se means 'through', but literally (word-by-word) means 'in from'.

Learn Urdu
3 November 2013 ·

Word of the day: dard - pain/ache

Usage: میرے سر میں درد ہے۔
Transliteration: mere sar meṇ dard he.
Translation: I have a headache.
Literally: my head in pain is.

Alternate: مجھے سر درد ہے۔
Transliteration: mujhe sar-dard he
Literally: to me head-ache is.

Learn Urdu
11 November 2013 ·

Word of the day: havā - air/wind

Usage: آج تیز ہوا چل رہی ہے۔
Transliteration: āj tēz havā chal rahi he.
Translation: There's a strong wind blowing today.
Literally: today fast air walk ing is.

Learn Urdu
16 November 2013 ·

Word of the day: jamna - to freeze

Usage: پانی جم کر برف بن گیا ہے۔
Transliteration: pāni jam ke barf ban gaya he.
Translation: The water has frozen into ice.
Literally: water freeze-by ice made is.

Learn Urdu
28 November 2013 ·

Word of the day: pighalna - to melt

Usage: برف گرمیوں میں پگھلتی ہے۔
Transliteration: barf garmioṇ meṇ pighalti he.
Translation: The ice melts in the summer.
Literally: ice summers in melts is.

Learn Urdu
10 December 2013 ·

Word of the day: uThna - to get up.

Usage: اس نے کہا، اٹھو-
Transliteration: us ne kaha, "uTho!"
Translation: he/she said, "get up!".
Literally: he/she ne* said, "get up!"

*ne is the transitive marker attached to the subject noun or pronoun for verbs in the past tense.

Learn Urdu
21 December 2013 ·

Word of the day: ţuuţna - to break - ٹوٹنا

Usage: اکبر بستر پہ لیٹا اور بستر ٹوٹ گیا-
Transliteration: akbar bistar pe leţa, aur bistar ţuuţ gaya.
Translation: Akbar lay on the bed and broke it.
Literally: akbar bed on lay and bed break went.

Learn Urdu
6 January 2014 ·

Word of the day: ţhanđ lagna - to feel cold

Usage: بارش ہونے کی وجہ سے مجھے اج بہت ٹھنڈ لگ رہی ہے۔
Transliteration: bārish hone ki vajah se mujhe āj bohot ţhanđ lag rahi he.
Translation: I feel cold today because of rain.
Literally: rain happening of-reason-from to-me today very cold feel-ing is.

Notes:

- bārish hona means 'to rain'. When there is a post position in front of the infinitive 'hona', it changes the ending of the infinitive to from 'a' to 'e'. So hona becomes hone.

- ki vajah se means 'due to' or 'because of'.

Learn Urdu
20 January 2014 ·

Word of the day: mehsuus karna - to feel - محسوس کرنا

Usage: لیزا آج اکیلا محسوس کر رہی ہے۔
Transliteration: Liza āj akela mehsuus kar rahi he.
Translation: Liza is feeling lonely today.
Literally: Liza today alone feel-ing is.

Note: تنہا (tanhā) can be used instead of akela as well.

Learn Urdu
23 January 2014 ·

Word of the day: saṛak - road - سڑک

Usage: جون سڑک پر گاڑی چلا رہا ہے۔
Transliteration: John saṛak par gāṛi chalā raha he.
Translation: John is driving a car on the road.
Literally: John road on car run-ning is.

Notes:
chalna means 'to walk'. chalāna means 'to make something walk' or 'to make something work/run'. gāṛi chalāna means 'to drive a car'.

Learn Urdu
27 January 2014 ·

Word of the day: havāi jahāz - aeroplane - ہوائی جہاز

Usage: وہ دیکھو ہوائی جہاز اڑ رہا ہے۔
Transliteration: vo dekho havāi jahāz uṛ raha he.
Translation: Look, there's an aeroplane flying
Literally: that look air ship fly ing is.

Note: havāi jahāz literally means air ship.

Learn Urdu
Published by Fahd Mir Jan [?] · 13 March 2014 ·

Word of the day: har koi - everyone - ہر کوئی

Usage: ہر کوئی تمہیں دیکھنا چاہتا ہے۔
Transliteration: har koi tumhe dekhna chahta he.
Translation: Everyone wants to see you.
Literally: everyone to-you to-see wants is.

Learn Urdu
Published by Fahd Mir Jan [?] · 13 March 2014 ·

Word of the day: har kisam - every type - ہر قسم

Usage: دنیا میں ہر قسم کے لوگ ہوتے ہیں۔
Transliteration: dunya meṇ har kisam ke log hote heṇ.
Translation: There are all kinds of people in the world.
Literally: world in all types of people exist are.

Learn Urdu
Published by Fahd Mir Jan [?] · 14 March 2014 ·

Word of the day: chīz - thing - چیز

Usage: مجھے وہ چیز چاہئے۔
Transliteration: mujhe vo chīz chahie.
Translation: I want that thing.
Literally: to-me that thing wanted.

Learn Urdu
Published by Fahd Mir Jan [?] · 29 May 2014 ·

Word of the day: us ke bād - after that - اس کے بعد

Usage: میں پہلے گھر جاؤں گا\جاؤں گی اور اس کے بعد مجھے باہر جانا ہے۔
Transliteration: meṇ pehle ghar jāunga/jāungi or us ke bād mujhe bāhir jāna he.
Translation: I will go (m/f) home first, and after that I have to go out.
Literally: I first home go-will and that-of-after to-me out to-go is.

Learn Urdu
Published by Fahd Mir Jan [?] · 30 May 2014 ·

Word of the day: phir - then - پھر

Usage: میں کھانے کے بعد پھل کھاؤں گا\گی اور پھر مجھے سونا ہے۔
Transliteration: meṇ khāne ke bād phal khāun gā/gi or phir mujhe sona he.
Translation: I'll have some fruit after lunch, and then I have to sleep.
Literally: I food of after fruit eat will and then to-me to-sleep is.

Note:
mujhe sona he in this post and mujhe bāhir jāna he in the previous post mean 'I have to sleep' and 'I have to go out' respectively. mujhe itself means 'to-me'. It is the dative case of meṇ (I). When the infinitive of a verb is placed between 'mujhe' and any 3rd person masculine form of the verb hona (to be), like 'he' (present), 'tha' (past), 'ho ga' (future) et al, the sentence implies that the verb has to be performed. An example with similar syntax to achieve this nuance can be found in Russian. мне пора идти could be translated as 'I have to go' or 'It is time for me to leave'. The мне is in the same dative case as mujhe is in Urdu, and идти (to go) is in the infinitive form.
Let's look at some more examples of this structure in Urdu using different tenses.

mujhe sona tha - I had to sleep.
mujhe sona hota tha - I had to be asleep.
mujhe sona ho ga - I will have to sleep.
mujhe subah jaldi uthna ho ga - I will have to wake up early in the morning.
mujhe khāna khāna he - I have to eat food. (khāna is both a noun and a verb)
mujhe kuch pīna he - I have to drink something.
tumhe jāna he? - you have to go?
usse chalna he - he/she has to walk (leave).
hameṇ parhna he - we have to sleep.
ap logoṇ ko jāna he? - you people have to go?
unheṇ kuch kehna he - they have to say something.

Note that in this structure, the form of 'hona' (to be) at the end of all these sentences is in the masculine 3rd person and it always remains so. Does not matter who is says it.

Learn Urdu
Published by Fahd Mir Jan [?] · 21 June 2014 ·

Word of the day: jo bhi ho - whatever happens - جو بھی ہو

Usage: جو بھی ہو، میں تمہارے ساتھ رہوں گی \ گا۔
Transliteration: jo bhi ho, meṇ tumhāre sāth rahuṇ gi / ga.
Translation: Whatever happens, I (f/m) will stay with you.
Literally: whatever happens, I (f/m) your side stay will.

Learn Urdu

Published by Fahd Mir Jan [?] · 13 July 2014 ·

Word of the day: badalna - to change - بدلنا

Usage: وہ کافی بدل گیا ہے پچھلے کچھ سالوں میں۔
Transliteration: vo kāfi badal gaya he pichhle kuchh sāloṇ meṇ.
Translation: He has changed quite a bit in the last few years.
Literally: He enough change (went) is last some years in.

Notes:
- kāfi means 'enough'. 'ye kāfi he' means 'this is enough'. However, kāfi is also used as 'quite a bit'.
- the 'gaya' in badal gaya adds a perfective aspect to the sentence. badal gaya gives the impression that the person in question has completed the process of changing.
- pichhla means 'previous', 'last'. The feminine form is 'pichhli' and plural is 'pichhle'.

Learn Urdu

Published by Fahd Mir Jan [?] · 22 August 2014 ·

Word of the day: arsa - (period of) time - عرصہ

Usage: بڑے عرصے بعد لرن اردو پر پوسٹ کر رہا ہوں۔
Transliteration: bare arse bād learn urdu par post kar rahā huṇ.
Translation: I'm posting on Learn Urdu after quite a while.
Literally: big time after learn urdu on post do-ing am.

Learn Urdu

Published by Fahd Mir Jan [?] · 26 August 2014 ·

Word of the day: mazāk - joke - مذاق

Usage: پاکستانی سیاست ایک مذاق بن گئی ہے۔

Transliteration: pākistāni siāsat ek mazāk ban gai he.

Translation: Pakistani politics has become a joke.

Literally: Pakistani politics one joke became is.

Note:

ban'na literally means 'to be made'. ban jāna is a composite verb that has the same route 'ban', but together with jāna (to go) it means 'to become'.

Learn Urdu

Published by Fahd Mir Jan [?] · 30 August 2014 ·

Word of the day: fārigh - free, unoccupied - فارغ

Usage: آج کل میں بلکل فارغ ہوں۔ میری چھٹیاں ہیں۔

Transliteration: āj kal meṇ bilkul fārigh huṇ. meri chhuttiāṇ heṇ.

Translation: I'm completely free these days. I'm on vacation.

Literally: today tomorrow I absolutely unoccupied am. my vacations are.

Notes:

- One day off is a chhutti. Multiple days off, vacations, holidays all can be translated to chhuttiāṇ.
- kal means yesterday as well as tomorrow. The difference in meaning is derived from the context. You can also think of kal as the days surrounding today. So āj kal would be something like 'today and the days surrounding today', which is similar to 'these days'.
- The word free has multiple meanings, and Urdu has a different word for each of those meanings. For example, free (as in freedom) is 'āzād', and free (as in download-this-movie-for-free) is 'muft'.

Learn Urdu

Published by Fahd Mir Jan [?] · 12 September 2014 ·

Vocabulary of the day: Colour - rang - رنگ (masculine noun)

White - safēd (سفید)
Black - kāla (کالا); siyāh (سیاہ)
Red - lāl (لال) and surkh (سرخ)
Blue - nīla (نیلا); Sky Blue - ferozi (فیروزی)
Green - sabz (سبز); harā (ہرا)
Yellow - zard (زرد); pīla (پیلا)
Orange - nāranji (نارنجی); orenj* (اورنج)
Pink - gulābi (گلابی); Rose - gulāb
Grey - salēti (سلیٹی); salēt comes from the English 'slate'.
Brown - khāki (خاکی); khāk - dirt, soil.
Purple - jāmani (جامنی); jāman is a purple coloured fruit.
Golden - sunehra (سنہرا); Gold - sona

*The English word Orange is more frequently used than nāranji in popular speech.

Learn Urdu
Published by Fahd Mir Jan [?] · 18 September 2014 ·

Vocabulary of the day: The human head - insāni sar - انسانی سر

Head - sar (masc) (سر)
Hair - bāl (masc pl) (بال)
Sideburns - kalmeṇ (fem pl) (قلمیں)
Forehead - mātha (masc) (ماتھا); peshāni* (fem) (پیشانی)
Eye - ankh (fem) (آنکھ) - ankheṇ (fem pl) (آنکھیں)
Eyebrows - bhaveṇ (fem pl) (بھویں)
Eyelashes - palkeṇ (fem pl) (پلکیں)
Ear - kān (masc) (کان)
Cheek - gāl (masc) (گال)
Nose - nāk (fem) (ناک)
Mouth - muṇ (masc) (منہ)
Tongue - zabān (fem) (زبان)
Tooth - dānt (masc) (دانت)
Chin - thorri (fem) (ٹھوڑی)
Neck - gardan (fem) (گردن)

Notes:

- peshāni is used in formal settings. The word is taken from Persian. mātha is the more commonly used word, originating from India.
- The words sar, bāl, kān, gāl, nāk, muṇ, and dānt remain the same in the nominative plural form. dānt can easily be remembered by association with the word 'dental' in English.
- The word zabān contains both the meanings found in the word tongue. So it also means language.

Learn Urdu
Published by Fahd Mir Jan [?] · 19 September 2014 ·

Vocabulary of the day: The human body - insāni jism - انسانی جسم

Head - sar (masc) (سر)
Neck - gardan (fem) (گردن)
Shoulder - kandha (masc) (کندھا); shāna (masc) (شانہ)
Chest - sīna (masc) (سینہ)
Arm - bāzu (masc) (بازو)
Armpit - baghal (fem) (بغل)
Elbow - kohni (fem) (کوہنی)
Hand - hāth (masc) (ہاتھ)
Wrist - kalāi (fem) (کلائی)
Palm - hathēli (fem) (ہتھیلی)
Finger - ungli (fem) (انگلی)
Thumb - angūTHa (masc) (انگوٹھا)
Nails - nākhun (masc) (ناخن)
Belly - pēt (masc) (پیٹ)
Navel - nāf (fem) (ناف)

Back - kamar (fem) (کمر); pusht (fem) (پشت)
Hip - kūlha (masc) (کولہا)
Thigh - rān (fem) (ران)
Leg - Tāng (fem) (ٹانگ)
Knee - ghuTna (masc) (گھٹنا)
Foot - pāuṇ (masc) (پاؤں); pēr (پیر)
Ankle - Takhna (masc) (ٹخنہ)

Learn Urdu
Published by Fahd Mir Jan [?] · 20 September 2014 ·

Word of the day: to argue - behes karna - بحث کرنا

Usage: میں تمہارے ساتھ بحث نہیں کرنا چاہتی\چاہتا۔
Transliteration: meṇ tumhāre sāth behes nahi karna chahti(f)/chahta(m).
Translation: I don't want to argue with you.
Literally: I your with argue not to-do want.

Learn Urdu
Published by Fahd Mir Jan [?] · 21 September 2014 ·

Word of the day: sāns lena - to breathe (lit. to take breath) - سانس لینا

Usage: وہ ابھی زندہ ہے۔ سانس لے رہا ہے۔
Transliteration: vo abhi zinda he. sāns le raha he.
Translation: He's still alive. He's breathing.
Literally: he now alive is. breath tak-ing is.

Note: sāns itself is a noun meaning 'breath'.

Learn Urdu
Published by Fahd Mir Jan [?] · 22 September 2014 ·

Vocabulary of the day: Months of the year - sāl ke mahīne - سال کے مہینے

The names of months in Urdu are taken from English and their pronunciations are adjusted to suit the Urdu speaker's accent.

January - janvari - جنوری
February - farvari - فروری
March - mārch - مارچ
April - aprēl - اپریل
May - maī - مئی
June - jūn - جون
July - julāi - جولائی
August - agast - اگست
September - satambar - ستمبر
October - aktūbar - اکتوبر
November - navambar - نومبر
December - disambar - دسمبر

Learn Urdu
Published by Fahd Mir Jan [?] · 26 September 2014 ·

Word of the day: khāndān - (extended) family - خاندان

Usage: میرا خاندان بہت بڑا ہے
Transliteration: mera khāndān bohot barra he.
Translation: my family is very big.
Literally: my family very big is.

Note:
- khāndān means extended family, including all your relatives.
- 'rr' will be used to transliterate retroflex 'r' from now on.

Learn Urdu
Published by Fahd Mir Jan [?] · 28 September 2014 ·

Vocabulary of the day: Body organs - jism ke azā - جسم کے اعضاء

Heart - dil (masc) (دل)
Brain - dimāgh (masc) (دماغ)
Spine - rirrh ki haddi (fem) (ریڑھ کی ھڈی)
Bone - haddi (fem) (ھڈی); haddiān (pl) (ھڈیاں)
Vein - rag (fem) (رگ); ragēṇ (pl) (رگیں)
Lung - phephrra (masc) (پھیپھڑا); phephrre (pl) (پھیپھڑے)
Rib - pasli (fem) (پسلی); pasliāṇ (pl) (پسلیاں)
Stomach - mēda (masc) (معدہ)
Liver - jigar (masc) (جگر)
Kidney - gurda (masc) (گردا); gurde (pl) (گردے)
Intestine - ānt (fem) (آنت); āntēṇ (pl) (آنتیں)

Learn Urdu
Published by Fahd Mir Jan [?] · 4 October 2014 ·

Word of the day: dard - pain/ache - درد

Usage: میرے پیٹ میں درد ہے۔
Transliteration: mere pett meṇ dard he.
Translation: I have a stomach ache.
Literally: my belly in pain is.

Note: You may replace the word pett with any other masculine noun used for a body part and the rest of the sentence would remain the same. If the noun is feminine, simply use meri instead of mere in the above sentence. For example, meri tāṇg meṇ dard he (lit. my leg in pain is).

Learn Urdu
Published by Fahd Mir Jan [?] · 5 October 2014 ·

Word of the day: gosht - meat - گوشت

Usage: میں زیادہ گوشت نہیں کھاتا/کھاتی۔
Transliteration: meṇ ziāda gosht nahi khāta(m.)/khāti(f.)
Translation: I don't eat meat a lot.
Literally: I much meat not eat.

Learn Urdu
Published by Fahd Mir Jan [?] · 8 October 2014 ·

Word of the day: jītna - to win - جیتنا

Usage: وہ مجھ سے کشتی میں جیت گیا۔
Transliteration: vo mujh se kushti meṇ jīt gaya.
Translation: He won a wrestling match with me.
Literally: he me-from wrestling in win went.

Learn Urdu
Published by Fahd Mir Jan [?] · 14 October 2014 ·

Word of the day: jurm - crime - جرم (Hindi: aprādh - अपराध)

Usage: چوری کرنا جرم ہے۔
Transliteratin: chori karna jurm he.
Translation: Stealing is a crime.
Literally: theft to-do crime is.

Learn Urdu
Published by Fahd Mir Jan [?] · 17 October 2014 ·

Word of the day: bīch meṇ - in between/in the middle of - بیچ میں

Usage: جان اور خان کے بیچ میں کون بیٹھا ہے؟
Transliteration: Jān or Khān ke bīch meṇ kon bettha he?
Translation: Who's sitting between Jan and Khan?
Literally: Jan and Khan of middle in who seated is?

Usage: "دیکھنا" اور "دکھانا" کے بیچ میں کیا فرق ہے؟
Transliteration: "dēkhna" or "dikhāna" ke bīch meṇ kia farq he?
Translation: What's the difference between "dēkhna" and "dekhāna"?
Literally: "dēkhna" and "dikhāna" of middle in what difference is?

Usage: وہ کمرے کے بیچ میں بیٹھا ہے۔
Transliteration: vo kamre ke bīch meṇ bettha he.
Translation: He's sitting in the middle of the room.
Literally: he room of middle in seated is.

Notes:
- dēkhna (infinitive) means 'to see'
- dikhāna (infinitive) means 'to show'

Learn Urdu
Published by Fahd Mir Jan [?] · 20 October 2014 ·

Vocabulary of the day: Vegetables - sabziāṇ - سبزیاں

Tomato - ttamāttar (masc.) (ٹماٹر)
Onion - piāz (masc.) (پیاز)
Garlic - lehsan (masc.) (لہسن)
Potato - ālu (masc.) (آلو)
Cucumber - khīra (masc.) (کھیرا)
Eggplant - beṇgan (masc.) (بینگن)
Green chilly - harī mirch (fem.) (ہری مرچ)
Paprika - surkh shimla mirch (fem.) (سرخ شملہ مرچ)
Capsicum - shimla mirch (fem.) (شملہ مرچ)
Turnip - shaljam (fem.) (شلجم)
Bitter gourd - karēla (masc.) (کریلا)
Ladies' fingers - bhinddi (fem.) (بھنڈی)
Coriander - dhanyā (masc.) (دھنیا)
Mint - podīna (masc.) (پودینا)

Learn Urdu
Published by Fahd Mir Jan [?] · 26 October 2014 ·

Vocabulary of the day: names of days - dinoṇ ke nām - دنوں کے نام

Monday - pīr (پیر)
Tuesday - mangal (منگل)
Wednesday - budh (بدھ)
Thursday - jumerāt (جمعرات)
Friday - juma (جمعہ)
Saturday - haftā (ہفتہ)
Sunday - itvār (اتوار)

Note: haftā can either mean 'week' or 'Saturday'.

Learn Urdu

Published by Fahd Mir Jan [?] · 12 November 2014 ·

Word of the day: sūṇghna (v.) - to smell (something) - سونگھنا

Usage: یہ خوشبو سونگھ رہی ہو؟
Transliteration: ye khushbū sūṇgh rahi ho?
Translation: Do you smell this aroma?
Literally: this aroma smell-ing are?

Notes: bū means a smell, and on its own it usually has a negative connotation. badbū translates to 'a bad smell' (bad is pronounced like the English 'bud', only with a dental 'd'), whereas khush means 'happy' and so khushbū is a nice smell - an aroma.

Learn Urdu

Published by Fahd Mir Jan [?] · 12 November 2014 ·

Text of the day:

بھارت کے شہر حیدرآباد میں اتوار کو بھارت اور سری لنکا کے درمیان تیسرے ایک روزہ کرکٹ میچ میں بھارت نے سری لنکا کو مسلسل تیسری مرتبہ شکست دے کر سیریز اپنے نام کر لی ہے۔

Transliteration:

bhārat ke shehr hedarabād meṇ itvār ko bhārat or sri lanka ke darmiān tīsre ek roza cricket match meṇ bhārat ne sri lanka ko musalsal tīsri martaba shikast de kar series apne nām kar li he.

Translation:

In the third one-day cricket match between India and Sri Lanka in the Indian city of Hyderabad, India defeated Sri Lanka for the third consecutive time and won the series.

Literally:

India-of city Hyderabad-in Sunday-on India and Sri Lanka of between third one day cricket match-in India (ne) Sri Lanka to constantly third time defeat give-by series self name got.

Vocabulary:
bhārat - India
shehr - city
darmiān - between
tīsra - third
musalsal - constantly
martaba - time (as in, 'how many times will you do that?')
shikast - defeat

Source: BBC Urdu

Learn Urdu
Published by Fahd Mir Jan [?] · 25 November 2014 ·

Word of the day: kis ka/ki/ke - whose - کس کا/کی/کے

Usage (ka): یہ گیند کس کا ہے؟
Transliteration: ye gēnd kis ka he?
Translation: Whose ball is this?
Literally: this ball who of is?

Usage (ki): یہ گھڑی کس کی ہے۔
Transliteration: ye gharrī kis ki he?
Translation: Whose watch is this?
Literally: this watch who of is?

Usage (ke): وہ جوتے کس کے ہیں۔
Transliteration: vo jūte kis ke heṇ?
Translation: Whose shoes are those?
Literally: those shoes who of are?

Note: The word 'who' is translated as 'kon' in the nominative case. In the oblique case (with a post-position), it becomes 'kis'. So before any post-position, 'who' is translated as 'kis'. Other examples are 'to whom' (who to - kis ko), 'from whom' (who from - kis se).

Learn Urdu
Published by Ali Ibrahim Rasheed [?] · 20 December 2014 ·

Word of the day: jānver - animal - جانور

Usage: پشاور کے سانحے کے بعد انسان اور جانور میں فرق محسوس نہیں ہوتا
Transliteration: Peshawar ke sānihe ke bād insān aur jānver meṇ farq mehsūs nahi hota
Translation: After Peshawar's incident, (you) don't feel the difference between man (human being) and animal.
Literally: Peshawar of incident of after man (human) and animal between difference feel not happens.

Learn Urdu
Published by Ali Ibrahim Rasheed [?] · 2 January 2015 ·

Word of the day: mehmān - guest - مہمان

Usage: کل میرے گھر مہمان آئے تھے۔
Transliteration: Kal mere ghar mehmān āe the.
Translation: Yesterday, guests came to my home.
Literally: Yesterday my home guests came.

Note(s):
- Based on the context, kal in this sentence is yesterday. Kal can also be used to indicate tomorrow.
- Plural of mehmān is also mehmān.
- āe because it's plural, also used for respect. Other forms are āya (for he), āi (for she). The 'y - ی' sound is more prominent when enunciating āya. Vo āya - he came. But diminished, almost negligible, in the other two cases.

Learn Urdu
Published by Ali Ibrahim Rasheed [?] · 11 February 2015 ·

Word of the day: gol - circular / round - گول

Usage: دنیا گول ہے۔
Transliteration: Duniya gol he.
Translation: (The) World is round.
Literally: World round is.

Note(s):
- Often used as a symbolic phrase with both positive and negative connotations. For instance, all good things must come to an end, because the world is round. Or, the bad days will surely pass, because the world is round. Etc.

Learn Urdu
Published by Fahd Mir Jan [?] · 18 February 2015 ·

Word of the day: dikhāna - to show - دکھانا

Usage: میں تمہے دکھاتی ہوں پیالی کہاں ہے۔
Transliteration: meṇ tumhe dikhāti huṇ piāli kahaṇ he.
Translation: I'll show you where the cup is.
Literally: I (to)-you show am cup where is.

Learn Urdu

Published by Ali Ibrahim Rasheed [?] · 9 March 2015 ·

Word of the day: kitāb - book - کتاب

Usage: فہد آج کل ایک کتاب لکھ رہا ہے۔
Transliteration: Fahd āj kal ek kitāb likh raha he.
Translation: Fahd is writing a book nowadays.
Literally: Fahd nowadays one book writing is.

Note(s):
- āj is today. kal is tomorrow or the day before.
- Together, āj kal means nowadays.

Learn Urdu
Published by Fahd Mir Jan [?] · 16 March 2015 ·

Vocabulary of the day: parinde - birds - پرندے

Following are birds common to the Indian Sub-continent.

Sparrow - chirria - چڑیا
Parrot - tota - طوطا
Hen - murghi - مرغی
Rooster - murgha - مرغا
Dove - fāxta - فاختہ
Pigeon - kabūtar - کبوتر
Peacock - mor - مور
Duck - batax - بطخ
Goose - murghābi - مرغابی
Swan - hans - گوڑا ہنس
Black Swan - siyah rāj hans - سیاہ راج ہنس
Eagle - okāb - عقاب
Kite - chīl - چیل

Ostrich - shatar murgh - شتر مرغ
Turkey - fīl murgh - فیل مرغ
Crow - kawwa - کوا
Falcon - bāz - باز
Quail - battēr - بٹیر
Heron - baglā - بگلا
Crane - sāras - سارس
Owl - ullu - الو
Cuckoo - koyal - کویل
Nightingale - bulbul - بلبل
Woodpecker - hudhud - ہدہد
Partridge - tītar - تیتر
Vulture - gidh - گدھ

Learn Urdu added a post from 26 March 2015 to their Timeline.
Published by Fahd Mir Jan [?] · 26 March 2015 ·

Vocabulary of the day: bimāriaṇ - ailments - بیماریاں

Fever - buxār - بخار
Cold - zukām - زکام
Flu - nazla - نزلہ
Itch - khujli - کھجلی
Headache - sardard - سردرد
Sprain - moch - موچ
Diarrhoea - dast - دست
Constipation - kabz - قبض
Paralysis - fālij - فالج
Heart Attack - dil ka dora - دل کا دورہ

Learn Urdu
Published by Fahd Mir Jan [?] · 27 March 2015 ·

Word of the day: marz (masc.) - illness, disease - مرض

Usage: یہ کس قسم کا مرض ہے؟
Transliteration: ye kis kisam ka marz he?
Translation: What kind of illness is this?
Literally: this which kind of illness is?

Note: Another word for illness is bimāri (femn.)

Learn Urdu
Published by Fahd Mir Jan [?] · 10 April 2015 ·

Word of the day: tabdīli (femn.) - change (n.) - تبدیلی

Usage: موسم میں تبدیلی آرہی ہے۔
Transliteration: mosam meṇ tabdīli ā rahi he.
Translation: A change can be seen in the weather.
Literally: weather in change come-ing is.

Learn Urdu
Published by Fahd Mir Jan [?] · 23 May 2015 ·

Word of the day: sālan - curry - سالن

Usage: آج کوفتے کا سالن بنا ہوا ہے
Transliteration: āj kofte ka sālan bana hua he.
Translation: Meatball curry is being served today.
Literally: today meatball of curry made is.

Learn Urdu

Published by Fahd Mir Jan [?] · 2 July 2015 ·

Vocabulary of the day: xāndān - family - خاندان

Urdu, like most South Asian languages, has a rich vocabulary when it comes to family relations. As you will see, these words cannot be accurately translated into English, as they lose their specificity.

Father - bāp باپ - valid والد
Mother - māṇ ماں - valda والدہ
Brother - bhāi بھائی
Sister - behn بہن
Son - betta بیٹا
Daughter - betti بیٹی
Paternal Grandfather - dādā دادا
Paternal Grandmother - dādi دادی
Maternal Grandfather - nāna نانا
Maternal Grandmother - nāni نانی

Father's Elder Brother - tāya تایا
Father's Elder Brother's Wife - tāi تائی
Father's Younger Brother - chachā چچا
Father's Younger Brother's Wife - chachi چچی
Paternal Aunt - phuphi پھوپھی
Paternal Aunt's Husband - پھوپھا
Maternal Uncle - māmuṇ ماموں
Maternal Uncle's Wife - mumāni ممانی
Maternal Aunt - xāla خالہ
Maternal Aunt's Husband - xālu خالو
Paternal Elder Uncle's Son (cousin) - tāya zād bhāi تایا زاد بھائی
Paternal Elder Uncle's Daughter (cousin) - tāya zād behn تایا زاد بہن
Paternal Younger Uncle's Son - chachera bhāi چچیرا بھائی
Paternal Younger Uncle's Daughter - chacheri behn چچیری بہن
Paternal Aunt's Son - phuphi zād bhāi پھوپھی زاد بھائی
Paternal Aunt's Daughter - phuphi zād behn پھوپھی زاد بہن
Maternal Uncle's Son - māmuṇ zād bhāi ماموں زاد بھائی
Maternal Uncle's Daughter - māmuṇ zād behn ماموں زاد بہن
Maternal Aunt's Son - xāla zād bhāi خالہ زاد بھائی
Maternal Aunt's Daughter - xāla zād behn خالہ زاد بہن

Brother's Son (Nephew) - bhatīja بھتیجا
Brother's Daughter (Niece) - bhatīji بھتیجی
Sister's Son (Nephew) - bhānja بھانجا
Sister's Daughter (Niece) - bhānji بھانجی
Brother's Wife - bhābhi بھابھی
Sister's Husband - behnoi بہنوئی
Grandson - pota پوتا
Granddaughter - poti پوتی
Husband - shohr شوہر - xāyand خاوند
Wife - bivi بیوی - begam بیگم - zoja زوجہ
Husband's Elder Brother - jetth جیٹھ
Husband's Elder Brother's Wife - jetthāni جیٹھانی
Husband's Younger Brother - devar دیور
Husband's Younger Brother's Wife - devrāni دیورانی
Husband's Sister - nand نند
Husband's Sister's Husband - nandoi نندوئی
Wife's Brother - sāla سالا
Wife's Brother's Wife - سالہار
Wife's Sister - sāli سالی
Wife's Sister's Husband - hamzulf ہم زلف

Spouse's Father - susar سسر
Spouse's Mother - sās ساس
Father of child's spouse - samdhi سمدھی
Mother of child's spouse - samdhan سمدھن

Note: The Urdu equivalent for 'great' in great-grandfather or great-grandson is 'par'. So great-grandfather becomes 'par dāda' and great-granddaughter becomes 'par poti'.

Learn Urdu
Published by Fahd Mir Jan [?] · 20 August 2015 ·

Word of the day: pakāna - to cook - پکانا

Usage: مجھے کھانا پکانے کا شوق ہے۔
Transliteration: mujhe khāna pakāne ka shok he.
Translation: I love cooking.
Literally: to me food to-cook of interest is.

Learn Urdu
Published by Fahd Mir Jan [?] · 21 August 2015 ·

Word of the day: pakna - to be cooked - پکنا

Usage: باورچی خانے میں کھانا پک رہا ہے۔
Transliteration: bāvarchixāne meṇ khāna pak raha he.
Translation: Food is being cooked in the kitchen.
Literally: Kitchen in food cook ing is.

Note: bāvarchi-xāna means kitchen. bāvarchi on its own means a cook/chef.

Learn Urdu
Published by Ali Ibrahim Rasheed [?] · 18 September 2015 ·

Word of the day: pāgal - mad person/crazy person - پاگل

Usage: سب پاگل کہتے ہیں کہ میں پاگل نہیں ہوں۔
Transliteration: sab pāgal kehte heṇ keh meṇ pāgal nahi huṇ.
Translation: All mad people say that I am not mad.
Literally: All mad people say that I mad not am.

Note(s): pāgal can be used in multiple contexts. To depict mental condition. Minor insult. In a playful manner.

Learn Urdu
Published by Ali Ibrahim Rasheed [?] · 17 October 2015 ·

Phrase of the day: mulk se bahir - out of country / to be abroad - ملک سے باہر

Usage: فہد آج کل ملک سے باہر ہے۔
Transliteration: Fahd āj kal mulk se bahir he.
Translation: Fahd is out of country nowadays.
Literally: Fahd nowadays country of out is.

Note(s):
āj and kal are two separate time denominators, today and tomorrow / yesterday respectively. But they are commonly used together to indicate a surrounding period of time such as "nowadays" or "these days".

Learn Urdu
Published by Fahd Mir Jan [?] · 26 January 2016 ·

Word of the day: jhandda - flag - جھنڈا

Usage: اس دفتر کے اوپر پاکستانی جھنڈا لہرا رہا ہے۔
Transliteration: us daftar ke ūpar pakistāni jhandda lehrā raha he.
Translation: The Pakistani flag is waving on top of that office building.
Literally: that office-of above pakistani flag wave-ing is.

Learn Urdu
Published by Fahd Mir Jan [?] · 27 January 2016 ·

Word of the day: chaman - garden - چمن

Usage: میں اپنی بیٹی کے ساتھ چمن میں سارا دن بیٹھی تھی۔
Transliteration: meṇ apni betti ke sāth chaman meṇ sāra din betthi thi.
Translation: I was sitting with my daughter in the garden all day.
Literally: I own daughter with garden in all day seated was.

Learn Urdu
Published by Fahd Mir Jan [?] · 1 February 2016 ·

Verb of the day: āna - to come - آنا

Usage: سردیاں آرہی ہیں۔
Transliteration: sardiāṇ ā rahi heṇ.
Translation: Winter is coming.
Literally: winters come ing are.

Note: The word sard (سرد) means cold and sardi (سردی) can be used for 'cold weather'. The word for the winter season in Urdu is sardiāṇ (سردیاں), which is the plural of 'sardi'. So winter is always treated as a plural in Urdu, as a collection of consecutive cold weather streaks. The same is true for summer in Urdu. garmiāṇ (گرمیاں) - summer(s) - is the plural of garmi (گرمی) - hot weather - which is in turn derived from the word garm (گرم) meaning hot.

Learn Urdu
Published by Fahd Mir Jan [?] · 2 March 2016 ·

Word of the day: khelna - to play - کھیلنا

Usage: میں کل سارا دن ٹینس کھیل رہا تھا\رہی تھی
Transliteration: meṇ kal sāra din ttenis khel raha tha(m)/rahi thi(f).
Translation: I was playing tennis all day yesterday.
Literally: I yesterday all day tennis play ing was.

Learn Urdu
Published by Fahd Mir Jan [?] · 3 March 2016 ·

Word of the day: nahāna - to bathe - نہانا

Usage: تم فون کیوں نہیں اٹھا رہی تھی؟ میں نہا رہی تھی۔ میں روز اس وقت نہاتی ہوں۔

Transliteration: tum fōn kiuṇ nahi uttha rahi thi? men nahā rahi thi. men rōz is vakt nahāti huṇ.

Translation: Why weren't you picking up the phone? I was bathing. I bathe daily at this time.

Literally: you phone why not pick ing were? I bath ing was. I daily this time bathe am.

Learn Urdu
Published by Fahd Mir Jan [?] · 20 April 2016 ·

Word of the day: sasta - cheap - سستا

Usage: آج کل تیل بہت سستا ہے۔
Transliteration: aj kal tēl bohot sasta he.
Translation: Oil is quite cheap these days.
Literally: today tomorrow oil very cheap is.

Note: For feminine nouns, the form is sasti (سستی) and saste (سستے) is used for nouns in plural form.

Learn Urdu
Published by Fahd Mir Jan [?] · 24 June 2016 ·

Word of the day: chhutti - holiday - چھٹی

Usage: پاکستان میں اتوار کے دن چھٹی ہوتی ہے۔
Transliteration: Pakistan meṇ itvār ke din chhutti hoti he.
Translation: Sunday is a holiday in Pakistan.
Literally: Pakistan in Sunday of day holiday happen is.

Learn Urdu

Published by Fahd Mir Jan [?] · 17 July 2016 ·

Word of the day: shabnam - dew - شبنم

Usage: صبح سویرے گھاس پر شبنم نظر آتی ہے۔

Transliteration: subah savere ghās par shabnam nazar āti he.

Translation: Dew appears early morning on the grass.

Literally: morning early (morning) grass-on dew (in) sight comes is.

Note: nazar āna is a compound verb meaning 'to appear' or 'to be visible'. It combines the the noun nazar (sight) and the verb of motion āna (to come). So 'to see something' translated into Urdu (kuch nazar āna) and translated back would be 'something comes (into one's) sight'.

Learn Urdu

Published by Fahd Mir Jan [?] · 18 July 2016 ·

Word of the day: sitāra - star - ستارا

Usage: کل رات آسمان صاف تھا۔ آسمان میں بہت سارے ستارے نظر آ رہے تھے۔

Transliteration: kal rāt āsmān sāf tha. āsmān meṇ boht sāre sitāre nazar ā rahe the.

Translation: The sky was clear last night. There were many stars in the sky.

Literally: yesterday night sky clean was. sky-in very many stars sight com-ing were.

Learn Urdu

Published by Fahd Mir Jan [?] · 19 July 2016 ·

Word of the day: jhandda - flag - جھنڈا

Usage: پاکستان کا جھنڈا سبز اور سفید رنگوں پر مشتمل ہے۔
Transliteration: pākistān ka jhandda sabz or safēd rangoṇ par mushtamil he.
Translation: The flag of Pakistan is composed of green and white.
Literally: pakistan-of flag green and white colours-on based is.

Notes:

- 'par mushtamil he' can mean 'is composed of' or 'is based on'.
- Another word for 'jhandda' is parcham.

Learn Urdu

Published by Fahd Mir Jan [?] · 20 July 2016 ·

Word of the day: sadar - (city) centre, president - صدر

Usage 1: میرا آج لاہور صدر میں کچھ کام تھا۔
Transliteration: mera āj lahor sadar meṇ kuchh kām tha.
Translation: I had some work in Lahore city centre today.
Literally: my today lahore centre in some work was.

Usage 2: پاکستان کے صدر کا نام ممنون حسین ہے۔
Transliteration: pākistān ke sadar ka nām mamnun husēn he.
Translation: The name of the President of Pakistan is Mamnoon Hussain.
Literally: pakistan-of president-of name mamnoon hussain is.

Learn Urdu
Published by Fahd Mir Jan [?] · 21 July 2016 ·

Word of the day: jazbāt - feelings, emotions - جذبات

Usage: میرا خیال تھا کہ وہ مجھ سے محبت کرتا تھا، لیکن وہ صرف میرے جذبات کے ساتھ کھیل رہا تھا
Transliteration: mēra xayāl tha ke vo mujh se mohabbat karta tha, lekin vo sirf mēre jazbāt ke sāth khēl raha tha.
Translation: I thought he loved me, but he was only playing with my feelings.
Literally: my thought was that he me-with love did (do was), but he only my feelings with play-ing was.

Learn Urdu
Published by Fahd Mir Jan [?] · 22 July 2016 ·

Word of the day: rāt - night - رات

Usage: میں کل رات سو نہیں سکی
Transliteration: meṇ kal rāt sō nahi saki (fem.)
Translation: I could not sleep last night.
Literally: I yesterday night sleep not could.

Learn Urdu
Published by Fahd Mir Jan [?] · 23 July 2016 ·

Word of the day: insāniat - humanity - انسانیت

Usage: عبدالستار ایدھی ایک پاکستانی تھا جس نے اپنی پوری زندگی لوگوں کی مدد میں وقف کر دی۔ اس کے لیے انسانیت سے زیادہ اہم اور کچھ نہ تھا
Transliteration: abdul sattar edhi ek pākistani tha jis ne apni pūri zindagi logoṇ ki madad meṇ vakf kar di. us ke lie insāniat se ziāda ahm ōr kuchh na tha.
Translation: Abdul Sattar Edhi was a Pakistani who spent his life helping people. Humanity, above all else, had the highest status in his life.
Literally: abdul sattar edhi a Pakistani was who his whole life people-of help-in dedication did. Him-for humanity-than more important else nothing was.

Learn Urdu
Published by Fahd Mir Jan [?] · 27 July 2016 ·

Word of the day: sēlāb - flood - سیلاب

Usage: پاکستان کے شمال میں بارشیں ہو رہی ہیں اور سیلاب آنے کا خطرہ ہے
Transliteration: pākistān ke shumāl meṇ bārsheṇ ho rahi heṇ ōr sēlāb āne ka xatra he.
Translation: The north of Pakistan is experiencing rain showers and there is a fear of floods.
Literally: Pakistan of North in rains happen-ing are and flood coming of fear is.

Learn Urdu
Published by Fahd Mir Jan [?] · 25 August 2016 ·

Word of the day: jalna - to burn or to be jealous - جلنا

Usage: میں نے چولہے پر کھانے کا خیال نہیں رکھا اور کھانا جل گیا۔
Transliteration: meṇ ne chūlhe par khāne ka xayāl nahi rakha or khāna jal gaya.
Translation: I did not keep an eye on the stove and the food got burnt.
Literally: I (ne) stove-on food-of care not kept and food burn went.

Usage: خان علی سے جلتا ہے کیونکہ علی ہر وقت دنیا کی سیر کر رہا ہوتا ہے اور خان کو کام سے کبھی فرصت نہیں ملتی۔
Transliteration: khān ali se jalta he kiuṇke ali har vakt dunia ki sèr kar raha hota hè or khān ko kām se kabhi fursat nahi milti.
Translation: Khan is jealous of Ali because Ali keeps traveling the world all the time and Khan never gets time off.
Literally: khan ali from jealous is because ali each time world of travel do ing is and khan to work from ever time-out not get.

Learn Urdu
Published by Fahd Mir Jan [?] · 26 August 2016 ·

Word of the day: larrna - to fight - لڑنا

Usage: گلی میں دو لڑکے لڑ رہے ہیں۔
Transliteration: gali meṇ do larrke larr rahe heṇ.
Translation: Two boys are fighting in the street.
Literally: street in two boys fight ing are.

Learn Urdu
Published by Fahd Mir Jan [?] · 18 August 2016 ·

Word of the day: aṇgrēzi - English - انگریزی

Usage: روزمرہ بولے جانے والی اردو میں اکثر انگریزی کے الفاظ استعمال ہوتے ہیں
Transliteration: rozmara bole jāne vāli urdu meṇ aksar aṇgrēzi ke alfāz istemāl hote heṇ.
Translation: English words are often used in everyday spoken Urdu.
Literally: everyday (routine) spoken urdu in often english of words used are.

Learn Urdu
Published by Fahd Mir Jan [?] · 8 September 2016 ·

Word of the day: burrha - old (man) - بوڑھا

Usage: ایک بوڑھا آدمی بوڑھی عورت کے ساتھ بات کر رہا تھا.
Transliteration: ek burrha ādmi burrhi orat ke sāth bāt kar raha tha.
Translation: an old man was talking to an old lady.
Literally: one old man old woman with talk do-ing was

Note: In some areas of Pakistan influenced by Panjabi, people say buda/budi instead of burrha/burrhi.

Learn Urdu
Published by Fahd Mir Jan [?] · 19 April 2017 ·

Word of the day: imkānāt - chances - امکانات

Usage: آج بارش کے امکانات ہیں۔
Transliteration: āj bārish ke imkānāt heń.
Translation: There are chances of rain showers today.
Literally: today rain of chances are.

Learn Urdu
Published by Fahd Mir Jan [?] · 14 April 2017 ·

Word of the day: pathar - stone - پتھر

Usage: میرے بیٹے کو چمن میں پتھر جمع کرنا پسند ہے۔
Transliteration: mére bétte ko chaman meń pathar jama karna pasand he.
Translation: My son likes to collect stones in the garden.
Literally: my son-to garden-in stones collect to-do likable is.

Learn Urdu
Published by Fahd Mir Jan [?] · 27 August 2017 ·

Word of the day: míttha - sweet - میٹھا

Usage: آج کل بازار میں بہت میٹھے تربوز اور آم مل رہے ہیں
Transliteration: áj kal bázár meñ boht mítthe tarbúz or ám mil rahe heñ.
Translation: There are some very sweet watermelons and mangos available in the market these days.
Literally: today tomorrow market in very sweet watermelons and mangos find ing are.

Notes: míttha is the masculine form of the word. Feminine form is mítthi and plural is mítthe. Both ám and tarbúz are the same in singular and plural forms. Urdu has many such nouns that do not change in the plural tense at all. The adjective (in this case mítthe) tells us that we mean the plural in this sentence.

Learn Urdu
Published by Fahd Mir Jan [?] · 30 April 2017 ·

Word of the day: vafadār - faithful/loyal - وفادار

Usage: میرا چوکیدار وفادار ہے۔ مجھے اس پر شک نہیں۔
Transliteration: mera chokidār vafadār he. mujhe us par shak nahi.
Translation: My security guard is loyal. I don't doubt him.
Literally: my guard loyal is. to-me him-on suspicion not.

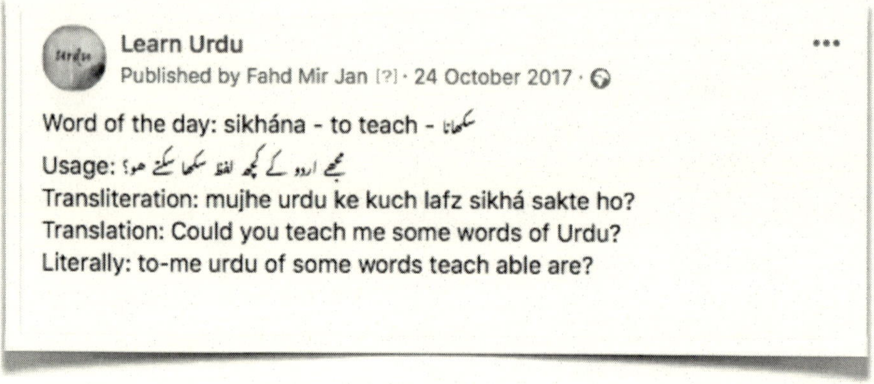
Learn Urdu
Published by Fahd Mir Jan [?] · 24 October 2017 ·
Word of the day: sikhána - to teach - سکھانا
Usage: مجھے اردو کے کچھ لفظ سکھا سکتے ہو؟
Transliteration: mujhe urdu ke kuch lafz sikhá sakte ho?
Translation: Could you teach me some words of Urdu?
Literally: to-me urdu of some words teach able are?

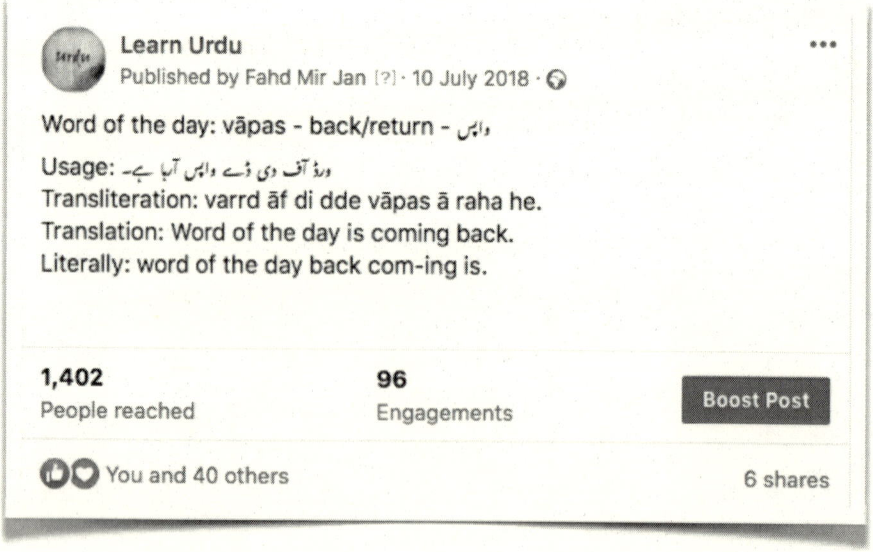
Learn Urdu
Published by Fahd Mir Jan [?] · 10 July 2018 ·
Word of the day: vāpas - back/return - واپس
Usage: ورڈ آف دی ڈے واپس آ رہا ہے۔
Transliteration: varrd āf di dde vāpas ā raha he.
Translation: Word of the day is coming back.
Literally: word of the day back com-ing is.
1,402
People reached
96
Engagements
Boost Post
You and 40 others
6 shares

Learn Urdu
Published by Fahd Mir Jan [?] · 12 July 2018 ·

Word of the day: jhīl - lake - جھیل

Usage: پاکستان کے شمال میں بہت ساری خوبصورت جھیلیں ہیں۔
Transliteration: pākistān ke shumāl meṇ boht sāri xubsūrat jhīleṇ heṇ.
Translation: There are several beautiful lakes in the north of Pakistan.
Literally: pakistan of north in very many beautiful lakes are.

1,539 People reached | **80** Engagements | Boost Post

46 | 2 comments 2 shares

Learn Urdu
Published by Fahd Mir Jan [?] · 15 July 2018 ·

Word of the day: rēt - sand - ریت

Usage: سمندر کنارے نرم ریت پیروں پے بہت اچھی محسوس ہوتی ہے۔
Transliteration: samandar kināre narm rēt pæroṇ pe boht achhi mehsūs hoti hæ.
Translation: Soft sand by the sea shore feels very pleasant to the feet.
Literally: sea shore soft sand feet on very good feel happens is.

1,619 People reached | **106** Engagements | Boost Post

48 | 2 comments 3 shares

Learn Urdu
Published by Fahd Mir Jan [?] · 18 July 2018 ·

Word of the day: rāz - secret - راز

Usage: وہ اپنا یے راز مرتے دم تک چھپائے گا۔
Transliteration: vo apna ye rāz marte dam tak chhupāe ga.
Translation: He will keep this secret of his until he dies.
Literally: he his this secret death breath till hide will

1,489
People reached

104
Engagements

Boost Post

51

4 shares

Learn Urdu
Published by Fahd Mir Jan [?] · 19 July 2018 ·

Word of the day: dikhāva - pretense/show - دکھاوا

Usage: جہان اس کی مدد صرف دکھاوے کے لئے کر رہا تھا۔
Transliteration: jahān us ki madad sirf dikhāve ke lie kar raha tha.
Translation: Jahan was helping him just for show.
Literally: jahan his of help only show of for do-ing was.

1,470
People reached

141
Engagements

Boost Post

72

23 comments 11 shares

Learn Urdu
Published by Fahd Mir Jan [?] · 16 January 2019 ·

Word of the day: samajhdār - smart - سمجھدار

Usage: میرے اسکول میں کئی سمجھدار بچے ہیں۔
Transliteration: mere askūl me kaī samajhdār bache heń.
Translation: There are several smart kids at my school.
Literally: my school in several smart children are.

1,216
People reached

69
Engagements

Boost Post

35

2 comments 3 shares

Learn Urdu
Published by Fahd Mir Jan [?] · 11 February 2019 ·

Word of the day: andāz - style/manner - انداز

Usage: مجھے اکرم کے بولنے کا انداز بہت پسند ہے۔
Transliteration: mujhe akram ke bolne ka andāz boht pasand hæ.
Translation: I love the way Akram speaks.
Literally: to-me akram-of speak-of manner very likeable is.

876
People reached

74
Engagements

Boost Post

34

5 comments 1 share

Learn Urdu
Published by Fahd Mir Jan [?] · 12 February 2019 ·

Word of the day: ganda - dirty - گندا

Usage: میری گاڑی گندی ہے۔ اسے صفائی کی ضرورت ہے۔
Transliteration: meri gāri gandi hæ. use safāi ki zarūrat hæ.
Translation: My car is dirty. It needs cleaning.
Literally: my car dirty is. to-it cleaning of need is.

Notes:
ganda گندا (m), gandi گندی (f), gande گندے (pl)

1,076
People reached

87
Engagements

Boost Post

34

3 comments 1 share

Learn Urdu
Published by Fahd Mir Jan [?] · 16 February 2019 ·

Word of the day: kamazkam - at least - کم از کم

Usage: مجھے کم از کم چار سیب چاہییں۔
Transliteration: mujhe kamazkam chār sēb chahieñ.
Translation: I need at least four apples.
Literally: to-me at-least four apples needed.

Notes:
kamazkam can also mean 'minimum'.

1,073
People reached

82
Engagements

Boost Post

36

8 comments 5 shares

Learn Urdu
Published by Fahd Mir Jan [?] · 17 February 2019 ·

Word of the day: mæhfūz - safe/secure - محفوظ

Usage: تمھارا راز میرے پاس محفوظ ہے۔
Transliteration: tumhāra rāz mere pās mæhfūz hæ.
Translation: Your secret is safe with me.
Literally: your secret my-near safe is.

Notes:
mere pās (my near) means 'near me' and is used for 'with me'.

1,073 People reached | 110 Engagements | Boost Post

50 | 24 comments 5 shares

Learn Urdu
Published by Fahd Mir Jan [?] · 25 June 2019 ·

Word of the day: khēt - field - کھیت

Usage: آج میں نے گندم کے کھیت میں ایک سانپ دیکھا۔
Transliteration: āj mæń ne gandam ke khēt mēń ek sāmp dēkha.
Translation: I saw a snake in the wheat fields today.
Literally: today I (ne) wheat of field in snake saw.

1,474 People reached | 108 Engagements | Boost Post

32 | 16 comments 1 share

Learn Urdu
Published by Fahd Mir Jan [?] · 24 July 2019 ·

Word of the day: żalabāri - hailstorm - ژالاباری

Usage: آج کراچی میں لوگ حیران ہیں کہ ساری رات ژالاباری ہو رہی تھی۔
Transliteration: āj karāchi meń lōg hærān hæń ke sāri rāt żalabāri ho rahi thi.
Translation: The people of Karachi were shocked today that there was a hailstorm last night.
Literally: today karachi-in people shocked are that all night hailstorm happen-ing was.

1,133
People reached

73
Engagements

Boost Post

31

10 comments

Learn Urdu
Published by Fahd Mir Jan [?] · 29 July 2019 ·

Word of the day: sūńghna - to smell - سونگھنا

Usage: آج باغ میں بچے گلاب کے پھول سونگھ رہے تھے۔
Transliteration: āj bāغ meń bache gulāb ke phūl sūngh rahe the.
Translation: Kids were smelling roses in the garden today.
Literally: today garden in kids rose of flowers smell ing were.

Notes: - غ is pronounced like the French 'r', but more guttural. It is usually romanised as 'gh', which can be confused with the aspirated 'g' - also written 'gh' by most. I'm going to write غ in the transliteration until I come up with a revised pronunciation guide that uses a different symbol for both the gh's.
- The plural of phūl (flower) is phūl.

Learn Urdu
Published by Fahd Mir Jan [?] · 31 August 2019 ·

Word of the day: magarmach - crocodile - مگرمچھ

Usage: مگرمچھ ایک بہت خطرناک جانور ہے۔
Transliteration: magarmach ek boht xatarnāk jānvar hæ.
Translation: Crocodiles are dangerous animals.
Literally: crocodile a very dangerous animal is.

1,019
People reached

67
Engagements

Boost Post

22

7 comments 1 share

Learn Urdu
Published by Fahd Mir Jan [?] · 16 September 2019 ·

Word of the day: tēz - fast - تیز

Usage: علی بہت تیز دوڑ رہا تھا۔
Transliteration: ali boht tēz dorr raha tha.
Translation: Ali was running very fast.
Literally: ali very fast run ning was.

1,043
People reached

50
Engagements

Boost Post

20

3 comments 1 share

Learn Urdu
Published by Fahd Mir Jan [?] · 1 October 2019 ·

Word of the day: pasandīda - favourite - پسندیدہ

Usage: پاکستان میں سردی میرا پسندیدہ مہینہ ہے۔ 😁
Transliteration: pakistan meń sardi mera pasandīda mahīna hæ.
Translation: Winter is my favourite month in Pakistan.
Literally: pakistan in winter my favourite month is.

992
People reached

47
Engagements

Boost Post

22

1 comment 1 share

Learn Urdu
Published by Fahd Mir Jan [?] · 2 October 2019 ·

Word of the day: sarrak - road - سڑک

Usage: مرغی نے سڑک کیوں پار کی؟
Transliteration: muryi ne sarrak kiūń pār kī?
Translation: Why did the chicken cross the road?
Literally: chicken ne road why cross did?

992
People reached

75
Engagements

Boost Post

12

7 shares

Learn Urdu
Published by Fahd Mir Jan [?] · 2 October 2019 ·

Word of the day: jūta - shoe - جوتا

Usage: کیا میرے جوتے ان کپڑوں کے ساتھ اچھے لگتے ہیں؟
Transliteration: kia mere jūte in kaprrōń ke sāth achhe lagte hæń?
Translation: Do my shoes look good with these clothes?
Literally: do my shoes these clothes of next-to good seem are?

1,010
People reached

42
Engagements

Boost Post

21

Learn Urdu
Published by Fahd Mir Jan [?] · 3 October 2019 ·

Word of the day: parvāh - care - پرواہ

Usage: مجھے کوئی پرواہ نہیں۔ میرا پیٹ بھرا ہوا ہے۔
Transliteration: mujhe koi parvāh nahi. mera pētt bhara hua hæ.
Translation: I don't care. I'm full.
Literally: to-me any care not. my belly full happened is.

Learn Urdu
Published by Fahd Mir Jan [?] · 4 October 2019 ·

Word of the day: sirf - only - صرف

Usage: کیا تم صرف اردو بولتے ہو؟
Transliteration: kia tum sirf urdu bolte ho?
Translation: Do you only speak Urdu?
Literally: do you only urdu speak are?

983
People reached

54
Engagements

Boost Post

18

5 comments 2 shares

Learn Urdu
Published by Fahd Mir Jan [?] · 5 October 2019 ·

Word of the day: kāsh - if only - کاش

Usage: کاش پرندوں کے پاس ہاتھ ہوتے۔
Transliteration: kāsh parindōń ke pās hāth hote.
Translation: I wish birds would have hands.
Literally: if only birds of near hands happened.

Learn Urdu
Published by Fahd Mir Jan [?] · 6 October 2019 ·

Word of the day: kitna - how much - کتنا

Usage: دکاندار کو: یہ انگوٹھی کتنے کی ہے؟ اور وہ ہار کتنے کا ہے؟ کل کتنا ہوا؟
Transliteration: dukāndār se: ye angūtthi kitne ki hæ? or vo hār kitne ka hæ? kul kitna hua?
Translation: To the shopkeeper: How much is it for this ring? And how much for that necklace? How much is it all together?
Literally: shopkeeper to: this ring how much of is? and that necklace how much of is? total how much happened?

1,155
People reached

48
Engagements

Boost Post

20

2 comments 1 share

Learn Urdu
Published by Fahd Mir Jan [?] · 8 October 2019 ·

Word of the day: xāmōsh - quiet - خاموش

Usage: ذرا خاموش رہو! میں سونے کی کوشش کر رہی ہوں۔
Transliteration: zara xāmōsh raho! mæń sone ki koshish kar rahi hūn.
Translation: Please be quiet! I'm trying to sleep.
Literally: little quiet be! I sleep of try do ing am.

951 People reached · 35 Engagements · Boost Post

16 · 1 comment 1 share

Learn Urdu
Published by Fahd Mir Jan [?] · 18 October 2019 ·

Word of the day: bahir - outside - باہر

Usage: باہر اندھیرا ہے اور بارش بھی ہو رہی ہے۔
Transliteration: bahir andhēra hæ or bārish bhi ho rahi hæ.
Translation: It's dark outside and raining as well.
Literally: outside dark is and rain too happen ing is.

1,148 People reached · 54 Engagements · Boost Post

27 · 6 comments 2 shares

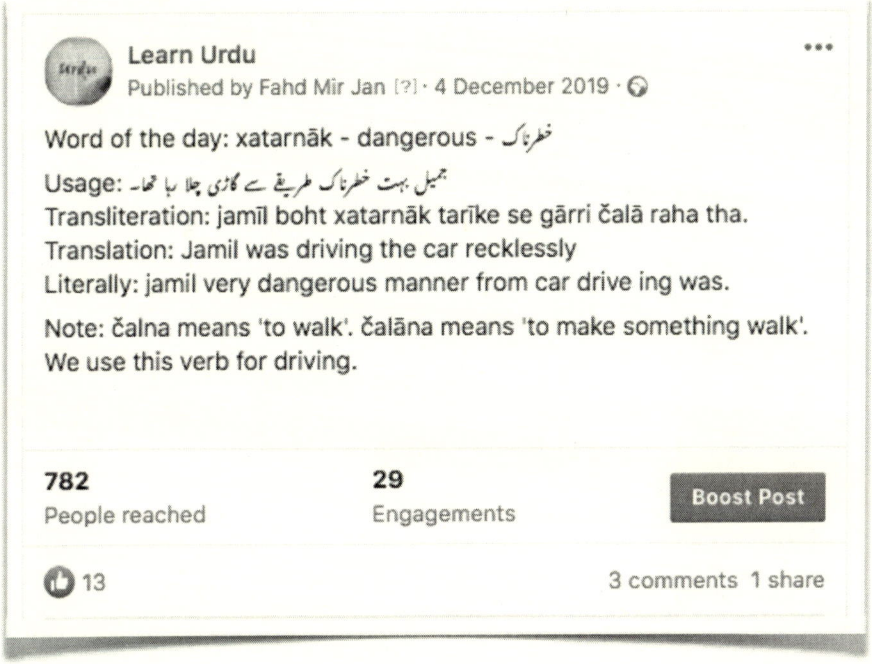
Learn Urdu
Published by Fahd Mir Jan [?] · 4 December 2019 ·

Word of the day: xatarnāk - dangerous - خطرناک

Usage: جمیل بہت خطرناک طریقے سے گاڑی چلا رہا تھا۔
Transliteration: jamīl boht xatarnāk tarīke se gārri čalā raha tha.
Translation: Jamil was driving the car recklessly
Literally: jamil very dangerous manner from car drive ing was.

Note: čalna means 'to walk'. čalāna means 'to make something walk'. We use this verb for driving.

782
People reached

29
Engagements

Boost Post

13

3 comments 1 share

Manufactured by Amazon.ca
Acheson, AB

12953562R00074